T0312267

Cambridge Elements ≡

Elements in New Religious Movements
edited by
James R. Lewis
Wuhan University
Rebecca Moore
San Diego State University

BRAINWASHING

Reality or Myth?

Massimo Introvigne
CESNUR, Center for Studies on New Religions

CAMBRIDGE
UNIVERSITY PRESS

CAMBRIDGE
UNIVERSITY PRESS

University Printing House, Cambridge CB2 8BS, United Kingdom

One Liberty Plaza, 20th Floor, New York, NY 10006, USA

477 Williamstown Road, Port Melbourne, VIC 3207, Australia

314–321, 3rd Floor, Plot 3, Splendor Forum, Jasola District Centre,
New Delhi – 110025, India

103 Penang Road, #05–06/07, Visioncrest Commercial, Singapore 238467

Cambridge University Press is part of the University of Cambridge.

It furthers the University's mission by disseminating knowledge in the pursuit of
education, learning, and research at the highest international levels of excellence.

www.cambridge.org
Information on this title: www.cambridge.org/9781009014632
DOI: 10.1017/9781009029568

© Massimo Introvigne 2022

This publication is in copyright. Subject to statutory exception
and to the provisions of relevant collective licensing agreements,
no reproduction of any part may take place without the written
permission of Cambridge University Press.

First published 2022

A catalogue record for this publication is available from the British Library.

ISBN 978-1-009-01463-2 Paperback
ISSN 2635-232X (online)
ISSN 2635-2311 (print)

Cambridge University Press has no responsibility for the persistence or accuracy of
URLs for external or third-party internet websites referred to in this publication
and does not guarantee that any content on such websites is, or will remain,
accurate or appropriate.

Brainwashing

Reality or Myth?

Elements in New Religious Movements

DOI: 10.1017/9781009029568
First published online: June 2022

Massimo Introvigne
CESNUR, Center for Studies on New Religions

Author for correspondence: Massimo Introvigne,
maxintrovigne@gmail.com

Abstract: The events of January 6, 2021 gave new currency to the idea of brainwashing. Some claimed that Trump's followers had been brainwashed, while others insisted that a "deep state" had brainwashed most Americans into accepting a rigged election. Scholars who explain that brainwashing theories have long been rejected by most academics and courts of law find it difficult to be heard. Brainwashing nevertheless remains a convenient explanation of how seemingly normal citizens convert to unusual religious or political ideologies. This Element traces its origins to the idea that conversion to deviant beliefs is due to black magic. A more scientific hypnosis later replaced magic and the Cold War introduced the supposedly infallible technique of brainwashing. From the 1960s, new religious movements, more commonly called cults, were accused of using brainwashing. Most scholars of religion reject the theory as pseudoscience, but the controversy continues to this day.

Keywords: brainwashing, mind control, mental manipulation, cults, new religious movements, cult controversies, cult wars

© Massimo Introvigne 2022

ISBNs: 9781009014632 (PB), 9781009029568 (OC)
ISSNs: 2635-232X (online), 2635-2311 (print)

Contents

Introduction   1

1 Free Will, Black Magic, and Hypnosis   3

2 Brainwashing and Cold War Propaganda   8

3 The Scientific Study of Communist Brainwashing: Lifton
  and Schein   25

4 The Cult Wars   32

5 Conclusion: Old Wine in New Bottles   58

  References   63

Introduction

On January 6, 2021, Trump supporters assaulted the US Capitol and interrupted a joint congressional session convened to certify Joe Biden's victory in the 2020 presidential elections. International media started paying more attention to a large network of conspiracy theorists called QAnon, which had played a role in preparing for the January 6 events.

One question many asked was: How was it possible that otherwise ordinary Americans, some with college degrees, followed QAnon and proclaimed their belief that the elections had been stolen by a cabal of corrupt politicians whose leaders worshipped Satan through pedophile rituals? One answer that emerged was that QAnon was a cult that used brainwashing to recruit followers. A larger pro-Trump network was also accused of using brainwashing. Activists who, since the 1970s, had accused new religious movements of gaining converts through brainwashing were interviewed by mainline media (see e.g., Milbank 2021). Sometimes they were taken more seriously than scholars who tried to explain that brainwashing theories had long before been rejected as pseudo-scientific by the majority of academics who had studied them.

Why do theories of brainwashing resurface so often? This Element explores the question historically. Since ancient times, all societies have considered certain forms of belief and behavior as deviant. They have asked why some individuals embrace doctrines and practices that the majority regard as strange, bizarre, heretical, or harmful. Section 1 shows that this question is old. Several ancient cultures believed that those who embraced deviant beliefs did not do so freely, but were manipulated by the gods, Fate, or evil humans through black magic. In the nineteenth century, the theory that those converting to deviant religions, including Mormonism, were manipulated through black magic was secularized by claiming that they were victims of hypnosis.

These theories, as discussed in Section 2, were not applied to aberrant beliefs in the field of religion only. Political ideologies were also targeted. From the 1920s, German Marxist and Freudian scholars tried to explain why, contrary to what their theories might predict, not only the bourgeoisie but a sizable number of blue-collar workers were enthusiastically joining the National Socialist Party. Their answer was that the Nazis had developed new effective techniques of mind control. After World War II, the same questions were raised in the United States with respect to Communism, an ideology also considered so absurd that no normal citizen would willingly embrace it.

While scholars struggled to confirm the existence of these techniques empirically, the Central Intelligence Agency (CIA), unencumbered by such scholarly subtleties, launched a massive propaganda effort to denounce mind control as allegedly practiced by the Soviets and the Chinese. The word "brainwashing" was coined in 1950 by Edward Hunter, a CIA agent who had a cover job as a journalist. Several publications followed. A popular 1959 novel, *The Manchurian Candidate*, adapted as a movie in 1962, made brainwashing a household word. To some extent, the CIA believed its own propaganda and tried to replicate the alleged Communist brainwashing through its own project, MK-ULTRA, with inconclusive results.

Section 3 follows the scholarly efforts of the 1960s to document brainwashing as reportedly practiced in China. Early on, scholars such as Robert Jay Lifton and Edgar Schein believed they had found some empirical evidence of the existence of unusual Chinese persuasion techniques. Lifton called them "thought reform," and Schein "coercive persuasion." The section also follows Lifton and Schein's subsequent careers, and their application of mind control models beyond Communist regimes.

In Section 4, I show how brainwashing theories were transferred from politics to religion by a leading British psychiatrist, William Sargant, who argued that mainline religions had learned to practice brainwashing long before Communism. Not surprisingly, Sargant's book did not please religionists. More popular was the theory developed in the 1970s by American psychologist Margaret Singer, which argued that not all religions, only cults, used brainwashing. Meanwhile, the proliferation of new religious movements in the United States and elsewhere had led to the creation of anticult organizations. They adopted the ideology of brainwashing and promoted the practice of deprogramming, aimed at reversing the brainwashing allegedly operated by the cults. The section follows the so-called cult wars, in which Singer and those who shared her theory – the anticultists and the deprogrammers – crossed swords with scholars of new religious movements. The latter argued that brainwashing was a pseudoscientific concept used to discriminate against unpopular religions. The opponents of brainwashing achieved important legal successes in the 1990s in the United States, although anti-brainwashing laws were passed in some European countries and Russia and China also officially adopted anticult theories.

Section 5 concludes the Element by showing that, while rejected by a solid majority of academic scholars of religion and American courts of law, brainwashing is still very much part of popular culture. It often resurfaces in media accounts of controversial religions. It has also emerged in new incarnations such as parental alienation syndrome (PAS) theory, which claims that one divorced parent often brainwashes children into hating the other parent. The events of January 6, 2021 showed how much brainwashing language is still with us, while some of those who stormed the Capitol also believed their critics were brainwashed.

While "cult" is a pejorative word that describes religions of which broader society disapproves, I will nevertheless use it throughout the Element because those who subscribe to brainwashing theories employ it. The distinction between legitimate religions, which do not utilize brainwashing, and cults, which supposedly do, is not part of accepted social science. The scholarly community that studies new and alternative religions ultimately rejected brainwashing theories, finding that they are circular. While proponents of brainwashing claim they are considering only deeds and bracketing creeds, in fact they are targeting unpopular beliefs. These theories claim that some groups are cults because they use brainwashing – sometimes called mind control, thought reform, coercive persuasion, menticide, and other euphemisms that basically have the same meaning. Proponents "know" that cults use brainwashing because nobody, without being brainwashed, would embrace the strange beliefs of these religions.

Scholars of new religious movements, including myself, who reject the theory of brainwashing are often accused by anticult activists of being cult apologists, for whom no cults are dangerous or criminal. Others see them as extreme cultural relativists who are persuaded that deviance is a purely subjective notion. I do not know any mainline scholar of new religious movements who would support this position. I myself created the category of "criminal religious movements" to designate religious groups that commit real crimes – such as terrorism, physical violence, pedophilia, and sexual abuse – as opposed to the imaginary crimes of being a cult or practicing brainwashing (Introvigne 2018). Criminal religious movements exist within both the oldest and the newest religious traditions. Pedophilia, for example, is statistically more prevalent in the Catholic Church and other mainline denominations than in new religious movements, although cases have been found in the latter as well (Shupe 1995, 2007).

I believe that criminal behavior should never be tolerated under the pretext of religious liberty. Criminals should be prosecuted. I also believe that chasing imaginary crimes often leads to overlooking real ones.

1 Free Will, Black Magic, and Hypnosis

The Search for Free Will

Every day, we are confronted with shocking news. A seemingly well-adjusted youth murders his parents. A model employee runs away with the company till. A promising graduate student drops out of college to become a full-time disciple of a controversial Eastern guru. We naturally wonder whether these acts derive, in fact, from free choices. Did that person really commit the act, or was she acted upon by external forces?

The question is not new. Greek tragedy suggested one possible answer: that we are not free but are instead like branches tossed about by a domineering wind called Fate or Destiny, or by the whims of unpredictable deities. Oedipus commits what to all appearances are horrible crimes, such as patricide and incest, yet Sophocles (497–406 BCE) suggests he is not guilty, having been deceived by Fate and the gods.

Asia had its own explanation of apparently absurd human actions and beliefs. They are the results of karma, an inexorable law causing our past lives, that we do not normally remember, to affect our present lives.

In several cultures, those who performed inexplicable deeds or embraced deviant beliefs were regarded as possessed by demons or evil spirits, or as victims of black magic performed by sorcerers. Others offered astrological determinism as an explanation, believing that stars can force people to a certain behavior.

If such is the case, humans are not ultimately responsible for their actions, and nobody should be punished by the law. The ancient Roman legal system solved the problem by maintaining that, when judged by courts of law, human actions should conventionally be considered as responsible acts imputable to their actors, no matter what their ultimate cause (Daube 1969). Let's imagine, for example, that Caius murdered his neighbor. Perhaps the ultimate reason for his actions stemmed from a joke that the supreme god Zeus played on him, or from Fate's inexorable web. The Roman judge, however, would not have been interested in such ultimate issues and would have attributed the proximate responsibility for the murder to Caius.

Christianity radically changed this state of affairs. After centuries of theological elaboration based on clear Jewish precedents, Christians, like Jews, regarded humans as fully responsible for their actions. Both the Christian doctrine of original sin and its New Testament interpretation stress that humans are free to choose between good and evil. Eventually, the Christian Church banned astrological determinism and doctrines of reincarnation. It did not ban belief in demons, however, but taught that if the Devil does tempt human beings, temptation can always be resisted. Thus, those who yield to temptation are guilty (Ogliaro 2003).

The triumph of this theory of free will was, however, short-lived. The crisis of the Middle Ages and the rise of Renaissance magic carried with them a return to astrological determinism and the belief that others can control our choices through black magic. Rationalism also raised its own doubts about free will.

One thinker who promoted such doubts was the English philosopher Thomas Hobbes (1588–1679), who was also the originator of the theory that certain religious choices are so strange that we cannot consider them as free. Well before Hobbes, many had suggested that deviant or heretical religions could not truly be embraced as the result of a free choice. Hobbes, however, widened the field to include any religion that went beyond a vague Deism (Hobbes 1651).

Hobbes' criticism of religion was continued by Anthony Ashley Cooper, the third Count of Shaftesbury (1671–1713), and by David Hume (1711–76), the leading British Enlightenment philosopher. Hume believed that psychology was the science to which religion, except perhaps the blandest form of liberal Christianity, must succumb (Yandell 1990). Most Enlightenment thinkers were not atheists. Rather, they followed Shaftesbury's distinction between a reasonable religion and a fanatical variety generating "pannick" (in modern English, panic: Shaftesbury 1708: 25), which was also adopted by Immanuel Kant (1724–1804) in his *Religion within the Bounds of Mere Reason* (Kant 1793).

Eventually, however, Kant's criticism of the "religion of fanatics" passed to Georg Wilhelm Friedrich Hegel (1770–1831) and opened the door to the philosophers of the so-called Hegelian Left. One of them, Ludwig Feuerbach (1804–72), was a self-professed atheist who proclaimed that religion was a "psychic pathology" (Feuerbach 1841: 89). Karl Marx (1818–83) tried to move Feuerbach's theory of religion into a more rigorous sociological context, by arguing that "religious consciousness" is a "product of society." But he still alluded to forms of manipulation hidden beyond religious belief and conversion in his famous formula that "religion is the opiate of the masses" (Marx 1844: 72).

Black Magic and Persuasion, West and East

While a post-Marxist critique of religion would suspect that all conversions have a pathological root, the idea that some religions are so abhorrent that it would be impossible for those in full possession of their mental faculties to freely embrace them is much more ancient. It is not by chance that Paul the Apostle (ca. 5–65 CE) said of Christianity that it was "foolishness to the Gentiles" (I Corinthians 1:23). Actually, Roman scholars did consider Christianity a form of madness, and believed that no solid Roman citizen would freely convert to the new religion. Early Christians were also suspected of secretly using black magic and spells to attract their converts (Stark 1996: 28–29). In turn, in the Middle Ages Christians accused heretics such as the Waldensians of the same black magic practices (de Lange 2000: 49).

As Michel de Certeau (1925–96) indicated, attributing bizarre beliefs to the effects of witchcraft and black magic was even more prevalent in the early modern era than in the Middle Ages, as confidence in free will had weakened (de Certeau 1990). That those professing peculiar beliefs had been bewitched by evil leaders skilled in sorcery was still a popular theory in eighteenth-century Italy, where otherwise skeptical philosophers continued to support it (Ferrone 1989).

The idea that witchcraft and sorcery explained conversions to heterodox religions was not only European. In China, the expression *xie jiao* was first used by Daoist Tang courtier Fu Ji (554–639 CE) to designate Buddhism, which he denounced as an evil heresy to be eradicated (Wu 2016: 8–9). Today Chinese anticult activists translate *xie jiao* as "evil cults," but Western and Chinese scholars agree that the translation is wrong and somewhat anachronistic (Palmer 2012; Zhang 2020).

Xie jiao, or heterodox teachings, have been identified since the seventh century CE as religious movements that threatened the stability and harmony of China. There were two main criteria that identified heterodoxy. The first to be labeled *xie jiao* were millenarian movements, which announced the end of this world and the imminent advent of a new era when a messianic figure – often, the movement's own leader – would replace the Emperor. Second, unlike legitimate religions *xie jiao* were accused of converting their followers through the use of black magic, with secret techniques involving spells, charms, magic mirrors, and poisons (Wu 2017: 57–92).

Apart from the very Chinese theory that the victims may be rescued through the use of "dog blood, a common method for dispelling sorcery" (Wu 2017: 63), the logic was not different from the one sustaining Western accusations that Waldensians and other heretics lured their followers through witchcraft.

Secularizing Black Magic: Conversion through Mesmerism and Hypnosis

Gradually, the black magic theory was secularized. As psychopathological explanations of religious conversion began to take hold, some started to argue that there were psychopaths who knew how to induce madness in their followers. The prophet of Islam, Muhammad, was offered as an example of such a dangerous psychopath. Writing in 1723 in the most influential English newspaper of the time, *The London Journal*, Thomas Gordon (1695–1750) described Muslims as fanatics "animated by a mad prophet, and a new religion, which made them all mad" (Gordon 1723). Soon, thanks to Franz Anton Mesmer (1734–1815), a mad prophet's power of converting his followers to madness and overcoming their free will took the new scientific name of Mesmerism or hypnotism.

A paradigm similar to hypnotism (the word hypnotism entered into common use much later) was already at work when critics tried to understand how apparently normal citizens converted to a strange new religion such as Mormonism, whose most scandalous feature was polygamy. At first, it was argued that Mormons converted their victims through black magic. Mary Ward – probably a pseudonym for Elizabeth Cornelia Woodcock Ferris (1809–93) – wrote that she based her report, *Female Life among the Mormons* (1855), on direct experience. She stated that the Mormon prophet Joseph Smith (1805–44) "exerted a mystical magical influence over me – a sort of sorcery that deprived me of the unrestricted exercise of free will" (Ward 1855: 38).

But we were then in the scientific nineteenth century, when sorcery was no longer an acceptable explanation of how respectable American women could be deprived of their free will. Thus, Ward's heroine was made to discover that the Mormons' secret weapon was what "is now popularly known by the name of Mesmerism." Joseph Smith "came to possess the knowledge of that magnetic influence, several years anterior to its general circulation throughout the country." Ward (1855: 230) added that the Mormon prophet "obtained his information, and learned all the strokes, and passes, and manipulations, from a German peddler, who, notwithstanding his reduced circumstances, was a man of distinguished intellect and extensive erudition. Smith paid him handsomely, and the German promised to keep the secret."

Historians of Mormonism failed to discover any evidence of a German peddler connected to Joseph Smith, but Mesmerism or hypnotism as secularized black magic became a common nineteenth-century literary device. Its most famous example is Svengali, the diabolical Jewish hypnotist of the 1894 novel *Trilby*. This novel, written and illustrated by a French-born cartoonist and novelist who lived in London, George du Maurier (1834–96), inaugurated the modern phenomenon of the bestseller (Pick 2000). Before becoming anathema today because of its antisemitism, the novel was made into several films in the twentieth century. Using his hypnotic powers, Svengali succeeds in turning a girl with no sense of melody into the greatest opera singer of all time. In the process, he subjugates her morally and sexually so completely that he eventually causes her death (du Maurier 1894).

In the nineteenth century, it gradually became a cliché to attribute conversions to new religions to Mesmerism. The Adventists, and the more enthusiastic among the Protestant revival movements, were among the religions so accused (Taves 1999: 132–35, 161–65). Mormons continued to be targeted as well (Givens 1997: 138). The hypnosis paradigm was linked to the fear of the

Other. The Mesmerist who allegedly taught the technique to the Mormons was a stranger, a German, reflecting the Otherness of the Mormon world view (Winter 1998), and Svengali was a Jew.

The definition of Otherness, however, varied with historical context. While it was the Methodists who mostly accused the Mormons of using Mesmerism, in the eighteenth century several patients (ninety-three in just one year in one single London hospital) had been admitted to English bedlams for a mental illness whose simple diagnosis was "Methodism" (Malony 1996: 20).

Anti-Mormonism also introduced another claim later used by anticultists, namely, that movements using hypnosis to convert their followers could not be bona fide religions. In 1877, in an article in the popular *Scribner's Monthly*, anti-Mormon John Hanson Beadle (1840–97) confessed that,

> Americans have but one native religion [Mormonism] and that one is the sole apparent exception to the American rule of universal toleration . . . . Of this anomaly two explanations are offered: one that the Americans are not really a tolerant people, and that what is called toleration is only such toward our common Protestantism, or more common Christianity; the other that something peculiar to Mormonism takes it out of the sphere of religion
>
> (Beadle 1877: 391).

Beadle's observation held the reader hostage, forcing him to conclude that Mormonism was not a religion. It was only by asserting that Mormonism was not really a religion that the image of the United States as the country of religious freedom could be reconciled with the American reality of anti-Mormon discrimination.

2 Brainwashing and Cold War Propaganda

Theories of Nazi Mind Control

Sigmund Freud (1856–1939) offered a novel contribution to the centuries-old negation of free will. While most human beings believe that their choices are free, they are, he argued, largely determined by the unconscious and by our forgotten childhood experiences.

Although Freud was also influenced by his family's Judaism, his opinions on religion were predominantly negative. For him, religion is the attempt to remain within a childish stage that is fixated on pleasure, rejecting pain and, with it, the real world. He wrote in *The Future of an Illusion* (1927) that religion was a neurosis, and a childish one at that.

Freud did not, however, believe that religious delusions always arise spontaneously. In most cases, they are instilled through effective techniques that fix their victims in a permanent state of infantilism. In his 1907 article, "About the

Sexual Enlightenment of Children," Freud approved the anticlerical measures introduced in France and hoped they would protect French children from the sinister techniques of indoctrination that he believed were used by the Catholic Church (Freud 1907).

Around 1920, three students of Freud, all socialist sympathizers, extended their teacher's critique of religious indoctrination to conservative politics. Paul Federn (1871–1950) was the first to define a psychoanalytical concept of authoritarianism in 1919 (Federn 1919), which came to be shared by Wilhelm Reich (1897–1957) and Erich Fromm (1900–80).

With Freud's support and approval, Federn, Reich, and Fromm further developed the concept of the authoritarian personality (Anthony 1996: 165– 77). They traced its origins primarily to sexual repression and authoritarian childhood education. The belief in an authoritarian worldview, they argued, is the product of a combination of a sadomasochistic predisposition formed in childhood with a cunning ideological indoctrination that manipulates it (Federn 1919; Reich 1933; Fromm 1941).

From 1929, Federn, Reich, and Fromm applied the authoritarian personality model to explain why so many Germans embraced the Nazi ideology. Although their conclusions did not exactly coincide, they all believed that the Nazis had developed a technique of highly effective psychological manipulation and used it on sexually frustrated German workers. This explained why, contrary to what Marxist theory would have predicted, millions of Germans from the working classes had been converted to Nazi ideology.

The idea that reactionary regimes use techniques to indoctrinate individuals who have been so predisposed by the repressive education they had received in childhood became a trademark theory of the so-called Frankfurt School, which proposed a combination of psychoanalysis and Marxism (Jay 1973). The Nazi regime persecuted the leaders of the Frankfurt School, both because they were anti-Nazi and because most of them were Jews. The school's leaders fled to the United States, where they further explored the manipulative psychological techniques believed to be used by Nazism and Fascism.

Stalinist Mind Control

After World War II, the United States turned from its anti-Nazi alliance with the Soviet Union to the Cold War. Communism was by then perceived as just as evil and illogical as Nazism. How seemingly reasonable citizens may become Communist needed to be explained, and it seemed natural to assume that the same sinister techniques of psychological manipulation once used by the Nazis to convert blue-collar progressive German workers into reactionary Third Reich warriors were known to the Soviets.

In fact, in the 1930s the spectacular trials that Lavrentiy Pavlovich Beria (1899–1953), the head of the People's Commissariat of Internal Affairs (NKVD), staged in the Soviet Union, with the defendants making inexplicable self-incriminating confessions, attracted the interest of the US and German intelligence services. They wondered whether Beria had discovered new persuasion techniques, and whether it would somehow be possible to learn what they were in order to use them for their own purposes. In the 1930s and 1940s, both the US and German intelligence services independently engaged in experiments that made use of hypnosis and drugs to enhance their persuasion capabilities (Scheflin and Opton 1978: 223–24).

In 1943, Canadian American psychologist George Hoben Estabrooks (1895–1973) wrote a book on hypnosis that would later be often quoted in support of brainwashing theories (Estabrooks 1943). In 1945, together with Richard Lockridge (1898–1982), a novelist, Estabrooks published *Death in the Mind*, a popular espionage novel that describes how the Nazis developed a secret weapon for the mental control of American military officers, who then committed unexplainable acts of sabotage (Lockridge and Estabrooks 1945). The secret Nazi weapon was very similar to what five years later would be attributed to the Communists, and identified by a new name – brainwashing.

Edward Hunter, the Inventor of Brainwashing

In 1949, two American academics, George Sylvester Counts (1889–1974) and Nucia Perlmutter Lodge, a Russian émigré (1894–1983), published a study of the Stalinist trials in which they accused the Soviet regime of widespread mind control of the Russian population and of attempting to export it to the West (Counts and Lodge 1949). In the same year, a novel by George Orwell (Eric Arthur Blair, 1903–50), *1984*, quickly became a best seller. It was a disturbing depiction of totalitarianism where, among other things, regime bureaucrats claimed that,

> We make the brain perfect before we blow it up. No one whom we bring to this place [the "Ministry of Love" facility, which serves as a concentration camp for dissidents] ever stands out against us. Everyone is washed clean. There is nothing left in them except sorrow for what they have done and love of the Party. It is touching to see how they love the Party. They beg to be shot quickly so that they can die while their minds are still clean
>
> (Orwell 1949: 113).

Orwell's fictional account made a deep impression on Edward Hunter (1902–78), a CIA agent whose cover job was that of a reporter, first with

English language publications in China and later at the *Miami Daily News*. Testifying before the House of Representatives Committee on Un-American Activities on March 13, 1958, Hunter repeated under oath that he had coined the expression brainwashing, which he had used for the first time in the *Miami Daily News* on September 24, 1950 after meeting a young Chinese man in Indochina. The man had used the expression *hsi nao* ("wash brain") when referring to what could happen in China "when somebody said something the Peiping Government wouldn't like" (Committee on Un-American Activities 1958: 14). However, Hunter also mentioned the "semantics of the Newspeak language described with such genius by George Orwell in his book, *1984*" (Committee on Un-American Activities 1958: 17). Indeed, Orwell's reference to a "brain [. . .] washed clean" was the most likely source for Hunter's invention of brainwashing rather than Chinese acquaintances (Anthony 1996: 69).

Around 1950, the CIA needed to explain why a significant number of apparently normal Westerners had accepted Communist ideology. Hunter played a useful role in offering brainwashing as an answer. Between 1951 and 1960, he published several books on the subject, in addition to giving lectures and testifying before Congress. His *Brain-Washing in Red China* (Hunter 1951), first published in 1951, was reprinted in 1953 to include an account of the Korean War. Known as a primer on brainwashing, the book is, for the most part, a reconstruction and a critique of the Chinese Communist propaganda found in literature, school textbooks, cartoons, and newspapers. In 1956, after the Korean War, Hunter published *Brainwashing: The Story of Men Who Defied It* (Hunter 1956), followed in 1957 by *The Story of Mary Liu* (Hunter 1957), and in 1958 by *The Black Book on Red China* (Hunter 1958).

Brainwashing: The Story of Men Who Defied It was purportedly written with the assistance of a Baltimore psychiatrist, Leon Freedom (1897–1969), and later reprinted in an expanded edition under a new title (Hunter 1960). More than *Brain-Washing in Red China*, the 1956 book extensively describes the mind control techniques that were allegedly being used by Russian and Chinese Communists. *The Story of Mary Liu* tells of a heroic Chinese woman who resisted brainwashing. *The Black Book on Red China* is an attack on the atrocities of the Chinese regime, with a chapter on brainwashing.

As was the case for many CIA agents, Hunter's retirement and the end of the hot phase of the Cold War was a cause of bitterness and disappointment, which led him to become a right-wing extremist. He privately published a magazine, *Tactics*, devoted to reiterating the kind of anti-Communist rhetoric for which he had been famous in the past. By the 1970s, it had become an anachronistic and marginal enterprise.

For Hunter, the main proof that Communists use brainwashing lies in the absurd nature of Marxist theories that are "so ridiculous and so patently false that an American would be inclined to laugh them off" (Hunter 1951: 224). Only brainwashing can explain why someone would accept them.

Hunter, however, made a distinction between brainwashing (hyphenated at first, later written as one word) and brain-changing. The first is "a system of befogging the brain so a person can be seduced into acceptance of what otherwise would be abhorrent to him" (Hunter 1956: 203). It is brought about by various kinds of pressure that might include beatings and threats, or simply the repetition ad nauseam of a propaganda message. For example, Hunter wrote that the repetition of Communist slogans to a driver who had been stopped in China for driving through a red light was "a form of brainwashing":

> Chiang Kai-shek [1887–1975, the Chinese nationalist leader who fled to Taiwan, from where he opposed the Communists] is no good; it is very bad to pass a red light; America is an imperialist aggressor nation; you should always watch out for red lights; Chiang Kai-shek is a bad bandit; and America is an aggressive, imperialist nation; next time, watch out for the red light
> (Hunter 1951: 144).

Hunter believed that brainwashing was universal in the Communist world. "A child has to begin indoctrination – brainwashing – from the cradle," he wrote, and "every man, woman, and child under communism must experience it" (Hunter 1956: 257). But this universal brainwashing was not irresistible: in China "the communist regime knows that vast numbers of people are waiting for the moment when open opposition will be practicable" (Hunter 1956: 278).

Brain-changing, however, is more sinister than brainwashing, Hunter explained. It is "the complete job in all its wickedness." "*Brain-changing* means alterations in thinking" (Hunter 1956: 233), brought about through the use of drugs, torture, and neurosurgery. After his early writings, however, Hunter realized that his promotion of the term brain-changing had not been successful, as nobody except himself was using it. He admitted that the word brain-changing "became obscured as *brainwashing* began to embrace all the available pressures that could be utilized to bend a man's will and change his attitudes fundamentally" (Hunter 1956: 233). Hunter's last book on the subject, *The Black Book on Red China*, listed "hunger, fatigue, tension, threats, violence, and on occasion even drugs and hypnotism" (Hunter 1958: 131) as constituent elements of brainwashing, while torture and drugs were only used in brain-changing.

On the cover of his 1956 book, brainwashing is defined as witchcraft and even a "black Mass" (Hunter 1956: 242) – black magic dressed in the modern garments of science "like a devil dancing in a tuxedo" (Hunter 1956: 4). Progressing through Hunter's writings, we find that this return to black magic language goes hand in hand with a growing alarm that "the danger now was not only from underestimating the effects of brainwashing, but of overestimating them!" (Hunter 1956: 12). In fact, Hunter insisted that individuals with strong religious beliefs, or a deep sense of patriotism, could resist brainwashing (although perhaps not brain-changing). For example, he reported that a group of Freemasons captured in the Korean War had succeeded in "keeping themselves whole" and operating a Masonic lodge, even while in jail, thus resisting brainwashing (Hunter 1956: 126).

Toward the end of his life, Hunter claimed that American prisoners in Vietnam had also been subjected to brainwashing programs. This time, they had resisted because, thanks to his books, brainwashing was now known to the American Army (Hunter 1975: 10).

Brainwashing and Menticide: Joost Meerloo

The CIA was aware that it needed scientific justification for theories that had, after all, been originally put forth by a humble newspaper reporter. For this reason, it researched European scholarly literature and, encountering the works of Dutch psychologist Joost Abraham Maurits Meerloo (1903–76), decided to support his research on brainwashing.

Meerloo offered a more scientific version of Hunter's brainwashing theory, introducing at the same time colorful expressions such as menticide (Meerloo 1951) and "rape of the mind." Meerloo's eclectic approach combined the theory of conditioned reflexes promoted by Soviet scientist Ivan Pavlov (1849–1936), Cold War propaganda, and psychoanalysis. The Dutch scientist studied Pavlov's famous experiments, in which a dog accustomed to hearing a bell ring every time it was given food then salivated when the bell rang but no food was served.

In 1944, when he was director of the psychology department in the Dutch government-in-exile in London, Meerloo had already accused the Nazis of using a propaganda technique based on mass hypnosis (Meerloo 1944: 38). The latter, he wrote in 1949, "can convert the civilized being into a criminal sleepwalker" (Meerloo 1949: 83). Later, in his major work, published in the United States in 1956 under the title *The Rape of the Mind* and in England in 1957 as *Mental Seduction and Menticide* (Meerloo 1956), Meerloo noted that Nazi brainwashing was less effective than the Soviet version because the Nazis had not applied Pavlov's techniques (Meerloo 1956: 48).

The distinction between brainwashing and menticide is not always clear in Meerloo's writings. Sometimes, he seems to consider brainwashing as a blander form of menticide, which is also at work in advertising and widespread in modern society; menticide is much more dangerous and may cause "psychic homicide," as the mind killers may lead the victims to suicide and death (Meerloo 1962: 93–97). Elsewhere, however, he used brainwashing and menticide synonymously (Meerloo, 1957: 91–92).

According to Meerloo, ancient cultures had an insight into brainwashing when they mentioned black magic and the evil eye (Meerloo 1971: 130). In modern times, however, "[n]o brainwashing is possible without totalitarian thinking" (Meerloo 1957: 106). In the end, Meerloo distinguished good from bad "Pavlovian" (i.e., mind control), based on the content of the implanted messages. "One suggestion [that] is not intended," he wrote, "is that Pavlovian as such is something wrong" (Meerloo 1957: 52), because it is at work every day in all forms of societies (Meerloo 1960). It becomes brainwashing or menticide only when used to promote totalitarian ideologies. Meerloo also cautioned about the use of theories of brainwashing by lawyers:

> The concept of brainwashing has already led to some legal implication, and these have led to new facets of imagined crime. . . . Several lawyers consulted me for information about clients who wanted to sue their imaginary brainwashers. The same concept . . . could be used maliciously to accuse and sue anybody who professionally gave advice to people or tried to influence them. . . . The shyster lawyer is now able to attack subtle human relationships and turn them into a corrupt matter . . . . What new possibilities for mental blackmail and sly accusation are open! (Meerloo 1957: 155–57).

Eventually, these cautious remarks were forgotten, and what remained of Meerloo's work was the fact that a distinguished European psychologist had given some credit to Hunter's brainwashing allegations. The CIA used this to bolster its own propaganda.

In a speech in May 1953 at a national meeting of Princeton University Alumni, Allen Welsh Dulles (1893–1969, 55), then CIA director, again claimed that only brainwashing could explain why people became Communists. Dulles said that Communists

> wash the brain clean of the thoughts and mental processes of the past and, possibly through the use of some "lie serum," create new brain processes and new thoughts which the victim, parrotlike, repeats . . . . The brain under these circumstances becomes a phonograph playing a disc put on its spindle by an outside genius over which it has no control (Dulles 1953).

The CIA continued to look for scholars ready to confirm these claims for many years. Eventually, it recruited a new generation of younger experts including University of Oklahoma psychiatrist Louis Jolyon ("Jolly") West

(1924–99), who went on to become director of the Department of Neuropsychiatry at the University of California at Los Angeles and later served as a link with the anticult movement (Marks 1979: 59).

A Brainwashing Manual

Scientology is perhaps the new religious movement most often accused of using brainwashing. It may thus seem surprising that in 1955 the Hubbard Association of Scientologists International – which served as the membership organization for the Church of Scientology until 1984 – published its own booklet titled *Brain-Washing: A Synthesis of the Russian Textbook on Psychopolitics*. Different theories point to the author as Scientology founder L. Ron Hubbard (1911–86), right-wing extremist Kenneth Goff (1909–72), or an anonymous American intelligence agent (Introvigne 2017).

Hubbard was familiar with Hunter's word "brainwashing," and in his 1951 book *Science of Survival* claimed to have uncovered a dangerous form of hypnosis called "pain-drug-hypnosis," which was similar to the Chinese brain-washing described by Hunter. Hubbard insisted that, "The extensiveness of the use of this form of hypnotism in espionage work is so wide today that it is long past the time when people should have become alarmed about it" (Hubbard 1951: 223).

In a 1956 lecture at the Games Congress – a conference he organized about game theory – Hubbard called Hunter's text on brainwashing "a fascinating book," revealing that he was familiar with the latter's claim that brainwashing originated from Pavlov (Hubbard 2005). At the Games Congress, Hubbard also made the surprising announcement that he was in possession of an obscure book allegedly written by Pavlov that included the most secret techniques of brainwashing:

> I happened recently to have gotten hold of the totality of information con-tained in the book written by Pavlov for Stalin and which hitherto has never been outside the doors of the Kremlin. I have that book. That book never left the Kremlin. Pavlov was not permitted to leave the Kremlin while he was writing that book and he was later more or less held in arrest, but he did not realize it to the end of his life (Hubbard 2005).

It is in this context that the 64-page booklet *Brain-Washing* was published in 1955. Shortly thereafter, Hubbard mailed it to the FBI and other federal agencies. The FBI's reaction was that,

> the authenticity of this booklet seems to be of a doubtful nature since it lacks documentation of source material and communist words and phrases. Also, there are no quotations from well-known communist works as normally

would be used in a synthesis of communist writings. In addition, the author
himself admits that he cannot vouch for the authenticity of this booklet
(SAC Los Angeles 1956).

Hunter did not welcome the competition and stated that "the book is a hoax,
and what it has mostly achieved is to fool people who think they are getting my
Brain-Washing in Red China which was based on first hand sources, and put the
word into the language" (Kominsky 1970: 544–45). On the other hand, the
evaluator at the Operations Coordinating Board of the National Security
Council wrote that "if the booklet is a fake, the author or authors know so
much about brainwashing techniques that I would consider them experts,
superior to any that I have met to date" (Seed 2004: 44).

On December 13, 1955, Hubbard wrote that "there is no political significance
attached to it [the booklet]. We couldn't be less interested [in politics], but
brainwashing happens to be a facet of the human mind and it has been necessary
to make available to our own people any and all texts which exist on the subject"
(Hubbard 1976: 310). In January 1956, Hubbard withdrew the *Brain-Washing*
booklet from circulation and asked that all copies be returned to Scientology,
following (or so he claimed) "the friendly opinion of the government" (Hubbard
1976: 328). Scientology never reprinted it.

Hubbard's *Brain-Washing* claims to be a synthesis of manuals circulated in
the Soviet Union by Beria before he was executed for treason in 1953 on
charges of selling Russian secrets to foreign intelligence agencies. The booklet
opens with a speech Beria allegedly gave to the "American students at the Lenin
University." After recalling a few fundamental principles of historical and
dialectical materialism, the speech embarks on a detailed discussion of psychopolitics and how pain-drug-hypnosis works. First, the subject is brought to the
point of an "artificial breakdown" using beatings and drugs. Then, through
hypnosis, the victim is "implanted" with specifically Communist content
(*Brain-Washing* 1955: 36)

In the 1950s, a frequent objection to brainwashing theories was that,
ultimately, persons under hypnosis would never act in ways radically contrary to their will or self-interest. According to the manual, this objection
was itself Communist propaganda, which "may be true of light, parlor
hypnotism: it certainly is not true of commands implanted with the use of
electric shock, drugs, or heavy punishment" (*Brain-Washing* 1955: 32–33).
A note on the back cover of *Brain-Washing* indicates that it was "published
as a public service by the Church of Scientology." An editorial comment was
signed by an unknown, and probably nonexistent, Professor Charles
Stickley.

One name not mentioned in the Scientology edition of the manual was Kenneth Goff, a former member of the US Communist Party in the 1930s who later converted to a fundamentalist and antisemitic form of Protestantism and became the leader of a Christian Identity educational facility, the Soldiers of the Cross Training Institute (Goff 1948). Goff claimed that before his conversion he had been "conditioned" to Communism by Soviet agents and knew brainwashing through direct experience (Goff 1954). He also insisted that he, rather than Hubbard, was the original compiler of *Brain-Washing* (Kominsky 1970: 547–49).

In 1970, Morris Kominsky (1901–75), a former Communist Party candidate for governor of Rhode Island in 1938, published a detailed study of *Brain-Washing* in his book *The Hoaxers*. Kominsky believed that the author of *Brain-Washing* was Goff. He included a letter in the book in which Goff insisted that he had privately circulated copies of the booklet before Hubbard published it (Kominsky 1970: 547–49), although Goff's edition was undated (Goff n.d.) and he could not supply any evidence of when it had been printed.

Opponents of the Church of Scientology believe that it is obvious that Hubbard authored *Brain-Washing*. For example, ex-Scientologist Bent Corydon regarded as conclusive a statement by Hubbard's son, L. Ron Hubbard, Jr. (Ron DeWolf, 1934–91), that "Dad wrote every word of it" (Corydon and Hubbard 1987: 108). Corydon also claimed that John Sanborn (1922–2011), who had assisted Hubbard in editing his works, recommended that a fake Soviet manual be produced connecting Communism with Scientology's worst foe, psychiatry, in order to discredit the latter. Hubbard then "disappeared into this little front room [of his home in Phoenix] which was sort of bedroom and study, and you could hear him in there dictating his book" (Corydon and Hubbard 1987: 108).

Hubbard reported his version of the origin of *Brain-Washing* in two of his *Operational Bulletins*, dated December 13 and 19, 1955. According to the second *Bulletin*, "fortuitously, in Phoenix there came into our hands two manuscripts . . . left there at the front desk with the request that they be mailed back to their owner" (allegedly "Charles Stickley") and "we are not sure exactly from whom these came." Subsequently, as the first *Bulletin* related, " Some of the mystery concerning the manuscript on brainwashing which came into our hands in Phoenix was resolved when it was discovered that a book called *Psychopolitics* (spelled with a K) is in the Library of Congress. It is in German. It was written by a man named Paul Fadkeller, and was published in Berlin in 1947" (Hubbard 1976: 309 and 312).

Hubbard added, "Although I may be misinformed, and I definitely do not read German, this book [*Brain-Washing*] is probably the Russian translation." He also noted in the second *Bulletin* that "we read it off onto a tape, compiling the two manuals and removing from them some of their very verbose nomenclature," and decided to publish the booklet as an aid to Dianetics auditors who might have to work with brainwashing victims (Hubbard 1976: 309 and 312).

On "Fadkeller," Hubbard was indeed misinformed. The actual name was Paul Feldkeller (1889–1972), and he was a German neo-Kantian philosopher. The only elements that his work (Feldkeller 1947), indeed published in Berlin in 1947 and a copy of which was in the Library of Congress, shares with *Brain-Washing* are some references to hypnosis and Nazi mass manipulation, and the use (but with a different meaning) of the term psychopolitics. Feldkeller's book is definitely not the German original of *Brain-Washing*.

That Hubbard wrote the booklet remains possible, perhaps even probable. An alternative possibility is that, given the interest of the American government and the CIA in the subject, a governmental agency prepared one or more manuscripts based on Soviet and American Communist tracts and Hunter's writings. The manuscripts were then forwarded, more or less anonymously, to Hubbard, and possibly to Goff as well. That the FBI doubted their authenticity does not exclude the possibility that the CIA might have produced them. Sometimes the FBI was not kept informed of the projects of the CIA or other agencies. The whole story of American intelligence involvement in the brainwashing controversy is so convoluted that this hypothesis cannot be excluded.

The reason why critics of Scientology insist that Hubbard wrote the booklet is that they claim it was later used as a manual to practice brainwashing in the Church of Scientology. The smoking gun, critics argue, is a July 22, 1956, *Technical Bulletin of Dianetics and Scientology* in which Hubbard claimed "We can brainwash faster than the Russians (20 secs to total amnesia against three years to slightly confused loyalty)" (Hubbard 1976: 474).

Critics read in these words an endorsement of brainwashing. On the contrary, however, Hubbard's works denounced brainwashing as something that should not be practiced, both on moral grounds and because it represents the triumph of everything Scientology found reprehensible and harmful in modern psychiatry. Hubbard also believed that brainwashing was useless, as it would reduce its victims to human shipwrecks, rather than converting them to new ideas.

I repeat that. It is not effective. It does not do a job. . . . It is a hoax – a hoax of the first order of magnitude. The Communist cannot brainwash anybody who is not [already] brainwashed. He cannot do it; he does not know how. It is one of these propaganda weapons. That's all it is. They [Communists] say, "We have this terrific weapon called brainwashing – we're going to brainwash everybody." Well, it would be awfully dangerous if they could. But do you know there is practically not a person in this room that would be permanently harmed by brainwashing, except as it related to being starved and kept under conditions of duress. In other words, if you put a guy into a military stockade and fed him poorly for two or three years, he is going to be in secondhand condition, isn't he? Well, that's just exactly the effect brainwashing had on them. It had no more effect than this (Hubbard 2005).

As we will see in the section "The CIA's Brainwashing Experiments: MK-ULTRA," the CIA experimented with brainwashing and came to the same conclusions as Hubbard. Brainwashing, or pain-drug-hypnosis, can destroy its victims, but not convert them to new beliefs.

The Manchurian Candidate

The Manchurian Candidate, a novel published by Richard Thomas Condon (1915–96) in 1959, was probably more influential than any nonfictional account of Communist mind control in making brainwashing a household concept in the United States and beyond. The 1962 film adaptation, directed by John Frankenheimer (1930–2002), was released at the height of tension between the United States and the USSR due to the Cuban missile crisis. (The 2004 remake, in which the Gulf War replaces the Korean War, drops the theme of Communist brainwashing.)

In the book, and in the 1962 movie, US sergeant Raymond Shaw (played by Laurence Harvey, 1928–73) and his unit under the command of Captain Ben Marco (played by Frank Sinatra, 1915–98) are captured by the North Koreans. Shaw is taken to a tent where the sinister Dr. Yen Lo drugs the whole American patrol and subjects them to hypnosis. In the movie, Yen Lo was portrayed by Khigh Alx Dhiegh (Kenneth Dickerson, 1910–91). The actor looked very much Asian but was in fact of mixed Egyptian and English ancestry, although he later founded a Taoist Sanctuary in Hollywood.

In the novel, Yen Lo organizes a demonstration of his results for the benefit of visiting Soviet KGB agents. The doctor's opening speech recaps the ideas on brainwashing that the CIA had disseminated. He reconstructs the origins of brainwashing in Pavlov's experiments. Yen Lo prefers to use the word conditioning, stating that it is "called brainwashing by the news agencies" (Condon

1959: 40) while in the movie he says that brainwashing is "the new American word" for the conditioning process.

Echoing Hubbard's *Brain-Washing*, but going further – in the novel physical pain is not mandatory and drugs are used only in the initial stage – Yen Lo states, "I am sure that all of you have heard that old wives' tale ... which is concerned with the belief that no hypnotized subject may be forced to do that which is repellent to his moral nature, whatever that is, or to his own best interests. That is nonsense, of course" (Condon 1959: 48). On the contrary, according to Yen Lo, given sufficiently advanced techniques, hypnosis could create unrepentant criminals.

The Communist doctor chooses Raymond Shaw because he is overwhelmed by resentment, which makes him an ideal candidate for brainwashing. He hates his mother for having deserted his father (who committed suicide) and having married Johnny Iselin, a corrupt senator. During Yen Lo's demonstration, Raymond is persuaded to strangle a fellow soldier and shoot another, for the sole purpose of demonstrating the effectiveness of brainwashing. The whole troop is then emptied of memories and led to believe that Raymond performed extraordinary acts of heroism to save them from overwhelming enemy forces. No violence, Condon insists, is involved, only a "deep mental massage" (Condon 1959: 34, 42). The whole process is accomplished in three days. Because of the brainwashing, the members of Raymond's patrol regard him as a hero, and he receives the Medal of Honor from the President's hands in a Washington ceremony.

Raymond is also manipulated by his devious mother (portrayed in the movie by Angela Lansbury, later of *Murder, She Wrote* fame), who wants to further her husband's political aims. But the Communists have different plans. Every time an American agent working for the Soviets invites Raymond to pick up a deck of cards for a game of solitaire, he reacts immediately as a result of his post-brainwashing state, which is permanent and irreversible. When he sees the queen of diamonds, he falls into a trance, ready to follow murderous instructions and then immediately forget his misdeeds. In this way, through a mysterious American agent who remains in the shadows, the Soviet KGB instructs Raymond to commit several murders.

In the end, though, Soviet plans do not work out as expected. Raymond meets his former commander, the now Major (and later Colonel) Marco. With assistance from the FBI, Army intelligence, and the CIA, Marco reconstructs the true sequence of events. However, even the best American experts cannot overturn Yen Lo's brainwashing, which is irreversible. Nor do they know all the details of the Communist plan, since they are unaware of a major element: The Soviet agent in Washington is none other than Raymond's mother. Her ultimate goal is to have Senator Iselin, her corrupt husband, win the vice presidential nomination, then have Raymond murder the presidential candidate and usher Iselin into the White House.

The plot thickens when Raymond's mother instructs him to murder the father of the girl he is in love with. Caught by the girl's mother, he kills her also. Because of the brainwashing, he immediately forgets the murders. Marco, however, tells him the truth, throwing Raymond into a state of utter despair. Nevertheless, through the usual queen of diamonds trick, Raymond's mother instructs him to ambush and kill the presidential candidate. Marco understands the plot, and tries to thwart it. In the end Raymond, an excellent sharpshooter, fires on the convention stage, but instead of targeting the presidential nominee he kills his stepfather and his mother. Then, following Marco's orders, he shoots again, killing himself. "No electric chair for a Medal of Honor Man," are Marco's final words (Condon 1959: 311). Marco was apparently convinced that a defense based on brainwashing would not have saved Raymond in an American jury trial.

Brainwashing and American POWs in the Korean War

Psychologist Dick Anthony popularized the expression "CIA brainwashing theory" to designate the version created by Hunter (and cautioned by Meerloo) that inspired Condon's novel and distinguish it from the academic studies of Lifton and Schein that we will examine in the next section (Anthony 1999). The CIA model included two stages. The first was called "softening up" by Hunter, and "deconditioning" by Meerloo. It called for emptying the brain of preexisting ideas, leading to a state of apathy induced by sleep deprivation, fatigue, hunger, and mistreatment. Physical pain was not always necessary. Meerloo insisted that inducing terror, fear, or despair sufficed to empty the brain and rape the mind, without need of physical violence or drugs (Meerloo 1957: 90). Once the brain was emptied, the second phase – the reconditioning performed through hypnosis – could begin, as it did in *The Manchurian Candidate*.

Hypnosis remains a rather vague concept in this literature. It could just be the obsessive reiteration of the same concepts that led to reconditioning. But Hunter presented the Communist lectures as almost miraculously effective. Why the lectures of Communist propagandists should be more successful at brainwashing than the no less boring or repetitive indoctrination of other ideologies was not explained. Again, we see a shift from an ostensibly neutral evaluation of techniques of brainwashing and menticide to a political value judgment on the absurdity of Communist doctrines.

In the CIA brainwashing theory, it went without saying that Communist brainwashing was based on Pavlov's famous experiments with dogs. The Pavlov connection was, however, disputed. Schein and his team (discussed in Section 3) wrote in 1961 that "in neither the Chinese nor the Soviet case has any evidence been turned up of any connection with Pavlovian psychology or any systematic use of his findings" (Schein, Schneier, and Barker 1961: 17). Others stated that when preparing prisoners for the show trials of the 1930s through "severe stress, sleep deprivation, and meticulous attention to reward and punishment," Stalin's prosecutors were indeed using findings by Pavlov (Dimsdale 2021: 32).

The CIA theory was also based on the idea that Chinese brainwashing techniques used against American POWs (prisoners of war) captured in the Korean War were remarkably effective, which was factually untrue. Hunter testified before Congress that "many" brainwashed American POWs "swallowed the enemy's propaganda line and declined to return to their own people" (Committee on Un-American Activities 1958: 15).

Albert D. Biderman (1923–2003), a psychologist with the US Air Force Scientific Research Office who wrote a report critical of Hunter, admitted that 39 percent of American POWs captured in Korea signed propaganda statements or letters in support of Communism (Biderman 1963: 38). However, at the end of the war, 4,449 American prisoners were given the choice of either returning to the United States or becoming citizens of China or another Communist country; only 21 (some 0.5 percent of the total) refused to return to their homeland (Biderman 1963: 30). This was not exceptional, Biderman wrote, since at the end of every war similar or higher percentages of POWs usually refuse to return home for a variety of reasons. As for the other 99.5 percent, clearly they had signed the statements to avoid mistreatment, without really believing them. If brainwashing was at work, a process with permanent effects on just half of 1 percent of the victims did not seem to be particularly effective.

Additionally, when their situation was reviewed a few years later, eleven of the twenty-one who had remained in China had asked for and received permission to return to the United States. Only ten had apparently become integrated in Chinese society (Pasley 1955). As scandalous as the choice of the "twenty-one who stayed behind" was for American public opinion, it did not constitute proof that Communist brainwashing worked. On the contrary, it demonstrated its failure.

North Korean and Chinese POWs who remained in American hands at the end of the Korean War were much more numerous than the American prisoners. Around 88,000 of them refused to go back to their homes in North Korea and China, preferring to stay in the West. Even if we take economic factors into account, the fact remains that a striking 51 percent of Chinese and North Korean prisoners refused repatriation, compared to 0.5 percent of American prisoners (Biderman 1963: 198–99). Perhaps capitalism was the real brainwashing.

The CIA's Brainwashing Experiments: MK-ULTRA

The CIA did not simply accuse Communists of brainwashing, knowing that this was propaganda produced by its own agents. It also tried to understand the true situation. Among other initiatives, in 1953 it commissioned Harold George Wolff (1898–1962), a Cornell University neurologist, and his colleague Lawrence Hinkle (1918–2012), to conduct a study on Stalinist Russia's techniques that had resulted in spectacular confessions in the Moscow show trials and their possible link to Chinese programs. The two authors published the study in 1956 in a scientific journal. They concluded that a public confession should not be confused with a genuine conversion, and that confessions in the Stalinist trials did not prove the effectiveness of brainwashing (Wolff and Hinkle 1956). In a sense, however, the CIA believed its own propaganda. It dreamed of creating its own Manchurian candidates by reproducing and improving the brainwashing techniques that were allegedly being used in China and Russia.

This project was code named MK-ULTRA. Originally, it was only mentioned in a handful of publications critical of the US government, and often dismissed as supporting conspiracy theories (Bowart 1978; Marks 1979; Gillmor 1987; Thomas 1989; Collins 1997). Later, however, the CIA became the defendant in several lawsuits, the most important of which resulted in a 1988 settlement. Through the lawsuits, several key documents became public (Bain 1976; Weinstein 1990; Collins 1997: 244–45). It was thus confirmed that, to further its brainwashing experiments, the CIA had secured the cooperation of several leading American universities and scholars, including Wolff, who were on the cusp of advanced research on behavioral sciences. Not all of them were fully aware of the ultimate aims of the project. The CIA concealed its involvement under three front foundations that were ostensibly private research organizations.

The first results were not encouraging. Each research team adopted one or more specific methods – such as hallucinogenic drugs, psychotropic medications administered in higher-than-normal doses, sensorial deprivation, repeated electroshock treatments, lobotomy and other forms of psychosurgery, and hypnosis. Some of the subjects were prison inmates, others were psychiatric patients of the researchers, or destitute volunteers who had been promised significant cash remuneration.

The CIA project took a quantum leap when Donald Ewen Cameron (1901–67), a distinguished Scottish psychiatrist who had been Professor of Psychiatry at McGill University in Montreal since 1943, joined the effort. Cameron would later become president of the American Psychiatric Association and found the World Psychiatric Association. In a protracted series of experiments on his Canadian patients, he combined many of the techniques that had formerly been tested separately. The CIA also appreciated that Cameron was working in Canada, thus circumventing legal restrictions forbidding such experiments in the United States and allowing the agency to funnel money into his research (Dimsdale 2021: 120–21).

Cameron based his experiments on a two-stage theory. In the first stage, which he called depatterning, he set out to eliminate the subject's existing ideas, habits, and attachments, generating a sort of selective amnesia. The outcome of this stage, in the words of a CIA executive, was the "creation of a vegetable" (Marks 1979: 142), not an especially useful subject for counter-espionage purposes. But then Cameron moved to the second stage that he called "psychic driving." Here, the subject was reconditioned to adopt new, permanent behavioral models and ideas.

In fact, Cameron was even too successful in creating vegetables. Some of the techniques he used included electroshock treatments that were between twenty and forty times stronger than the average doses administered in psychiatric hospitals. He gave them to the patients three times a day for several days. He also administered medication to induce sleep deprivation for periods of fifteen to sixty-five days. He gave his patients cocktails of psychotropic prescription medicine and hallucinogens, in quantities much higher than in their normal recreational use. Not surprisingly, as court cases were to reveal in later years, most of the patients succumbed to mental and other illnesses and never recovered. Some died.

Moreover, the passage from depatterning to psychic driving never succeeded. Cameron recorded on tape his own instructions, as well as phrases spoken by the patient. The vegetable-like patients produced by the depatterning were compelled to listen to the tapes for up to sixteen hours a day. Sometimes, microphones were inserted in football helmets that patients could not remove. Microphones were also hidden under their pillow, so they could continue to listen to the tapes even in their sleep. But nothing worked.

If anything, Cameron's experiments proved that brainwashing a victim into changing her fundamental ideas or orientation was not possible. Having reached the same conclusions, the CIA ended the MK-ULTRA project, including the part that Cameron had conducted, in 1963 (Marks 1979: 144–45). To use Hunter's unfortunate metaphor, the CIA learned that it might be possible to wash the brain until it loses its color and becomes white, as the patient is reduced to the sad state of a human wreck. But recoloring it with new ideas is not possible.

3 The Scientific Study of Communist Brainwashing: Lifton and Schein

Erik Erikson and Totalism

While the CIA promoted a somewhat primitive theory of brainwashing for propaganda and military purposes, other branches of the US government supported the work of credentialed academics who studied the persuasion techniques allegedly used by the Chinese. They came from the tradition of the Frankfurt School, and were all indebted to the recently proposed theory of totalism.

In the early 1950s, psychoanalyst Erik Erikson (1902–94) developed his concept of totalism, which encompassed totalitarian personalities irrespective of their right- or left-wing beliefs (Erikson 1954). According to Erikson, the unresolved crises of childhood development coupled with an authoritarian education play a key role in the origin of totalism. The propaganda spun by political and religious totalitarian ideologues skillfully manipulates these predispositions, although for Erikson it does not create them.

Psychological manipulation techniques, Erikson insisted, do not convert everybody to totalistic ideologies. They work only on those who are already predisposed to such a conversion because of their childhood experiences (Erikson 1954, 1956; Anthony 1996: 182–206; Murariu 2017: 73–92). These principles guided the scholars commissioned by the US government to study brainwashing as allegedly practiced in China and North Korea.

Robert Jay Lifton: Totalism and Thought Reform

An author frequently quoted in the debate about brainwashing is American psychiatrist Robert Jay Lifton. His work owes much to Erikson's concept of totalism. Lifton's book *Thought Reform and the Psychology of Totalism: A Study of "Brainwashing" in China* was originally published in 1961. Apart from the book's title, he rarely used the word brainwashing and always put it in quotation marks. He reported the results of his study of twenty-five Westerners who had been detained in Chinese Communist jails and fifteen Chinese who had also undergone thought reform processes, but outside of prisons. Referring frequently to Erikson, Lifton described Chinese thought reform as a totalistic technique more extreme than the Soviet or Nazi routines discussed in earlier debates on manipulation.

However, Lifton did not present the Chinese Communist brainwashing as infallible. Of the forty subjects he studied, only two retained a more favorable attitude toward Communism after their release and emigration than they had before their indoctrination. It was true that all forty subjects had signed pro-Communist statements. In most cases however, the acceptance of Communist ideology turned out to be either false or short-lived, induced by fear of punishment. Once they were at a safe distance from their reformers, most prisoners promptly rejected Communism.

In two cases out of forty, however, and perhaps in another four not included in his final study for lack of sufficient information, Lifton found something approaching a long-lasting conversion to Communism. Quoting Erikson, he explained it as a predisposition to totalism, perhaps derived from childhood problems.

> In all cases of apparent conversion (the two I studied in detail, the two I met briefly, and two others I heard of) similar emotional factors seemed to be at play: a strong and readily accessible negative identity fed by an unusually great susceptibility to guilt, a tendency toward identity confusion … a profound involvement in a situation productive of historical and racial guilt, and finally, a sizable element of totalism (Lifton 1961: 131).

Chapter 22 of Lifton's book was often quoted in subsequent brainwashing controversies. Here, he identified the causes of conversion to political or religious totalitarian ideologies in the interaction of three elements: a philosophical motivation, a psychological predisposition, and totalitarian manipulation techniques. "They require, rather than directly cause, each other," he claimed (Lifton 1961: 420). A philosophical motivation is indeed the starting point. "Behind ideological totalism," Lifton wrote, "lies the ever-present human quest for the omnipotent guide – for the supernatural force, political party, philosophical ideas, great leader, or precise science – that will bring ultimate solidarity to all men and eliminate the terror of death and nothingness" (Lifton 1961: 436).

Not all those who look for ultimate meaning embrace totalistic ideologies and the question why some do "raises the most crucial and the most difficult of human problems," Lifton suggested. He was not convinced that a single answer could explain all cases and focused his attention on "factors in one's personal history." "It may be that the capacity for totalism is most fundamentally a product of human childhood itself, of the prolonged period of helplessness and dependency through which each of us must pass" (Lifton 1961: 436–37).

Totalitarian ideologues know how to manipulate these predispositions. They use, Lifton argued, eight themes. The first theme is that of Milieu Control, understood as "control of human communication," isolation, and removal of any interaction with the outside environment. The second, Mystical Manipulation of emotions, plays on trust and mistrust, alternating them. The third theme is Demand for Purity, an obsessive distinction between the pure and the impure which leads to feelings of guilt and shame since complete avoidance of contact with the impure is impossible. The fourth theme is the Cult of Confession, which asks that contacts with impure persons and thoughts are confessed. The fifth is Sacred Science, whereby the totalitarian ideology is introduced as absolute scientific truth. Ultimately, the ideology is God, and denying it is both immoral and unscientific, which is especially important since our modern age puts such a premium on science. The sixth theme is Loading the Language with strong emotional overtones, which reiterate the distinction between good and bad in every conversation. The seventh is the predominance of the Doctrine over the Person; people are no longer defined by their humanity, but with reference to ideological clichés. An individual is regarded either as a proletarian or as an enemy of the people, rather than as a person first and then categorized politically. The eighth and final theme is Dispensing of Existence, whereby human life is no longer deemed to be important. The ideology therefore counts more than the person, an easy justification for all sorts of crimes (Lifton 1961: 419–35).

Hundreds of books and articles have applied Lifton's eight themes to religious cults. He regarded this application as feasible (Lifton 1987a: 209–19), although he also warned that some totalistic features are present in all religions. He also noted that in certain circumstances even a "full-blown totalist milieu" may offer positive rather than damaging experiences (Lifton 1961: 435).

Lifton insisted that Milieu Control, which implies a physical separation of the individual from his surrounding society, is "the most basic feature of the thought reform environment." It requires "group process, isolation from other people, psychological pressure," as well as "geographical distance or unavailability of transportation, and sometimes physical pressure" (Lifton 1987a: 212). The Chinese Communists were only occasionally successful in their thought reform program, with a mere 5 percent of the individuals Lifton analyzed showing any signs of long-lasting conversion. This relative lack of success was even more remarkable because, in addition to controlling prisons and concentration camps, the Chinese also controlled thousands of square miles of surrounding territory, thus giving the physical and geographical impression of total control (Lifton 1961: 420).

Obviously, a religious movement would only rarely replicate similar conditions, although it may create totalistic islands within nontotalistic societies (Lifton 1987a: 213). Lifton did not like cults, but believed they were a cultural rather than a medical or legal problem.

> Cults are not primarily a psychiatric problem, but a social and historical issue . . . . I think that psychological professionals can do the most good in the area of education. I myself feel critical of much of the totalistic inclination in many cults, but I do not think that pattern is best addressed legally . . . . Not all moral questions are soluble legally or psychiatrically, nor should they be (Lifton 1987a: 218–19).

As to the term brainwashing, Lifton suggested that scholars "do not use the word *brainwashing* because it has no precise meaning and has been associated with much confusion" (Lifton 1987a: 211).

Throughout his career, Lifton continued to be concerned with the subject of totalism and thought reform, which he saw at work in Communism and Nazism (Lifton 1987b), but also in the Western obsession with nuclear weapons (Lifton and Falk 1982) and the American defense of the death penalty against European objections. Later, Lifton defined religious fundamentalism as "the most extreme expression of totalism" (Almqvist and Wallrup 2005: 3).

According to Lifton, contemporary cults are either totalistic or fundamentalist in varying degrees, but are also capable of evolving over time to become nontotalistic and non-fundamentalist (Lifton 1987a: 219). Lifton studied Aum Shinrikyo, the Japanese new religion responsible for the March 1995 deadly sarin gas attack in a Tokyo subway and other serious crimes. He recognized that there is a "controversy surrounding the use of the word *cult* because of its pejorative connotation, as opposed to the more neutral *new religion*" (Lifton 1999: 11). He advocated using the term cult to identify those "groups that display three characteristics: totalistic or thought-reform-like practices, a shift from worship of spiritual principles to worship of the person of the guru or leader, and a combination of spiritual quest from below and exploitation, usually economic or sexual, from above" (Lifton 1999: 11).

Scholars of Asian religions criticized Lifton's book on Aum Shinrikyo, noting that guru worship is an intrinsic feature of many religious movements regarded as perfectly legitimate in Asia. They also noted that lack of familiarity with Japanese language sources led Lifton to portray an image of Aum Shinrikyo as somewhat monolithic and fixed in time, while the movement went through deep changes throughout its history. Different categories of members had different experiences. One well-known scholar of Japanese religion called the book "woefully undocumented," noting that "much written in this book about Aum and Japan will strike some as not quite right if not in fact wrong" (Gardner 2001: 126).

More generally, Lifton often expressed his personal disapproval of cults because they were at odds with his liberal political ideas. He insists that the mark of a balanced personality is its openness to diversity, change, and ambiguity, which he believed was lacking in the black-and-white world of cults. On the other hand, he did not believe that all cults present a threat to society, nor should they be suspected of potentially lethal criminal actions and kept under watch by law enforcement. Only what he called "world-destroying cults" should be the object of such surveillance (Lifton 1999: 202–3).

World-destroying cults such as Aum Shinrikyo, Lifton wrote, are not simply totalistic. They promote "a vision of an apocalyptic event or series of events that would destroy the world in the service of renewal," and an "ideology of killing to heal, of altruistic murder and altruistic world destruction." Their leaders easily succumb to the "lure of ultimate weapons," including nuclear weapons and toxic gas. And in Aum Shinrikyo Lifton saw an "extreme technocratic manipulation" that went beyond his model of thought reform by using powerful hallucinogenic drugs (Lifton 1999: 202–13).

Lifton realized that few cults can be compared to Aum Shinrikyo, and suggested that law enforcement should concentrate on identifying which cults are or can become world-destroying, separating them from the broader field of totalistic movements that use forms of thought reform that are unpalatable but not, in his opinion, illegal (Lifton 1999: 329).

Edgar Schein and Coercive Persuasion

In 1961, the same year as Lifton's *Thought Reform and the Psychology of Totalism* was published, Edgar H. Schein and his team published another important study of Communist persuasion techniques. The son of a Jewish Hungarian academic who escaped first from Stalinist Russia and later from Czechoslovakia just before the Nazi invasion, Schein was exposed from his early youth to the horrors of twentieth-century totalitarianism (Schein 1993). After migrating to the United States, he gained a psychology degree from Harvard University. He then served in the US army as a psychologist. In 1953, he was sent to Korea to examine POWs that China and North Korea had released to the United States, and who had reportedly been subjected to brainwashing.

Schein studied popular brainwashing theories but found them esoteric, because they called into play mysterious, unknown forces to explain processes of persuasion that, he believed, could be explained more simply. He thus became "a spokesperson for this more common-sense way of looking at the Korean prisoners of war episode" (Schein 1993: 39). Schein concluded that Chinese and North Korean persuasion tools did not differ from other known techniques. Additionally, they were not highly effective. Most POWs, like those submitted to Chinese thought reform in Lifton's studies, had merely stated that they believed in Communism in order to survive, without experiencing a genuine conversion (Schein 1956; Schein, Schneier, and Barker 1961: 8, 18). In fact, he regarded the experiences of American businessmen and missionaries who had been jailed under China's thought reform campaigns, and subsequently released, as more interesting than the Korean POWs for evaluating the effectiveness of Communist indoctrination. In 1961, Schein's research on the topic was included in *Coercive Persuasion*, which he co-wrote with two colleagues after he had retired from military life and joined Massachusetts Institute of Technology in 1956 (Schein, Schneier, and Barker 1961).

In *Coercive Persuasion*, Schein and colleagues criticized the brainwashing theories developed by the CIA, referring to them as demonology (Schein, Schneier, and Barker 1961: 254). They did not believe brainwashing, as understood in popular literature, to be a scientific theory, claiming that it referred to mysterious forces whose very existence could not be demonstrated. *Coercive Persuasion* tackled two major issues. The first was the relationship between conformity and conversion; the second, the connection between persuasion techniques and the contents of the message. The case of the POWs and others who signed statements in favor of Communism, but repudiated them once liberated, was an instance of conformity rather than conversion. Conformity, Schein and colleagues argued, is common, while conversion is rare. They claimed that in the sample they examined there were no genuine conversions to Communism obtained through brainwashing, not even a single case (Schein, Schneier, and Barker 1961: 164–65).

And yet, for Schein, the simple distinction between conformity and conversion "is not sufficiently sophisticated," and did not exhaust the analysis of Chinese thought reform. What happens in a totalitarian environment such as Communist China is "that the sphere of private activity becomes restricted or eliminated, that the belief system becomes ritualized and comes to serve solely an adjustment function, and that such ritualization may leave the individual without the cognitive tools to lead a creative private life" (Schein, Schneier, and Barker 1961: 267).

Schein did not suggest that, after a period of time, private thoughts end up conforming to public acts. Rather, he thought that in a totalitarian environment the distinction between public and private disappears. Ironically, he noted, this is not a good result for the totalitarian institution that initiated the process: "It may lead to a ritualization of belief and a gradual atrophy of creative abilities, which presumably the institution wishes to preserve and harness toward its own goals" (Schein, Schneier, and Barker 1961: 285).

The second issue discussed in the 1961 book is whether the coercive persuasion – the expression Schein used to avoid the demonological word brainwashing (Schein, Schneier, and Barker 1961: 18) – practiced in Communist China differs from other forms of indoctrination that are customarily accepted and practiced in the West. These include indoctrination and propaganda in schools, prisons, military academies, Catholic convents and monasteries, the marketing of certain products, and corporate life. If a difference exists, Schein asked whether it lies in the method of persuasion or, rather, in the contents of the indoctrination.

To answer this question, Schein and colleagues developed a three-stage framework of coercive persuasion: "unfreezing" the former identity, "changing" it, and "refreezing" a new identity. Fueling the process are feelings of guilt and the identification with a person who is looked upon as a role model. False information is also supplied. However, "coercive persuasion involves no more or less of such distortion than other kinds of influence, but our popular image of 'brainwashing' suggests that somehow the process consists of extensive self-delusion and excessive distortion. We feel that this image is a false one" (Schein, Schneier, and Barker 1961: 239).

Schein agreed with Lifton and Erikson that an identity crisis and "childhood conflicts, particularly around problems of authority" (Schein, Schneier, and Barker 1961: 145) are useful tools for identifying those with a predisposition toward embracing totalitarian ideologies. He also agreed that past political ideas may be relevant (Schein, Schneier, and Barker 1961: 252). Unlike Lifton, however, Schein rejected the idea that coercive persuasion or thought reform is fundamentally different from forms of persuasion practiced daily in Western societies and regarded as fully legitimate. "Chinese Communist coercive persuasion is not too different a process in its basic structure from coercive persuasion in institutions in our own society which are in the business of changing fundamental beliefs and values" (Schein, Schneier, and Barker 1961: 282).

It could be claimed that Western institutions such as "educational institutions, religious orders, AA [Alcoholics Anonymous], psychoanalysis, revival meetings, fraternities, and so on ... are entered voluntarily and ... the individual may withdraw voluntarily" from them, unlike Chinese prisons. While this is true, Schein argued that in Western institutions "the social pressures which can be generated can be as coercive as the physical constraints" of the Chinese jails (Schein, Schneier, and Barker 1961: 275).

In later works, Schein studied aspects of corporate life such as IBM's Sands Point Center in New York, whose goal was to transform executives into full-time "IBM men," and General Electric's Indoctrination Center whose name, as Schein noted, spoke for itself. He concluded that corporate indoctrination was similar to Chinese thought reform. Salaries – "golden handcuffs" – and the fear of being fired were just as intimidating as the physical walls of the Chinese prisons (Schein 1993: 44). When we disapprove of Communist coercive persuasion while admiring the very same methods at work in the training of Catholic nuns, the rehabilitation of prison inmates, or international corporations, Schein concluded, we may believe that we are, respectively, censuring or approving a technique, but in reality we are judging results rather than being concerned about the methods used to achieve them.

Unlike Lifton, who believed that thought reform was mostly a morally deplorable process, Schein argued that coercive persuasion could be acceptable and even socially useful. In the conclusion to the 1961 book, Schein and his colleagues wrote that,

> there is a world of difference in the content of what is transmitted in religious orders, prisons, educational institutions, mental hospitals, and thought reform centers. But there are striking similarities in the manner in which the influence occurs, a fact which should warn us strenuously against letting our moral and political sentiments color our scientific understanding of the Chinese Communist approach to influence (Schein, Schneier, and Barker 1961: 285).

Schein's later career was living proof of this conclusion. He decided to focus his studies on the psychology of corporate management, working both as a college professor and a consultant to leading European and American corporations. He did not consider managers' indoctrination through coercive persuasion to be a negative phenomenon. On the contrary, he assisted corporations in perfecting their techniques, although he also insisted that they should not try to absorb individuals' identities into the corporate one. By doing so, they would inhibit the managers' creativity to the ultimate detriment of the corporation (Schein 1985). Coercive persuasion by Chinese Communists was bad, Schein argued, while coercive persuasion by IBM, General Electric, and other corporations he worked for was good – not because the persuasion techniques were different, but because they were used to persuade people to adopt different beliefs and lifestyles.

4 The Cult Wars

Brainwashing Meets Religion: William Sargant

In the view of several scholars of totalism, many religious organizations were totalistic. These scholars came from a psychoanalytic tradition generally suspicious of, if not outright hostile to, religion since the days of Freud. While studies supported by the CIA or the US government did not include slandering religion among their purposes, the terminology of brainwashing was first systematically applied to religious conversion by English psychiatrist William Walters Sargant (1907–88).

Sargant had conducted studies on the mental problems of English soldiers during World War II. In 1944, he discovered Pavlov and, as he narrated in his 1967 autobiography, while reading some religious writings in his father's house he noticed that "all these books reported changes in brain function similar to those we had witnessed while abreacting [reliving] severe war neuroses and to those that Pavlov had noted in his terrified dogs" (Sargant 1967: 116). Several years later, he witnessed various religious revivals in the United States and found a confirmation of his 1944 intuition. Later on, in 1957, when he was convalescing in Majorca after a bout of tuberculosis, he wrote and published *Battle for the Mind: A Physiology of Conversion and Brainwashing* (Sargant 1957). The book was to sell more than 200,000 copies (Sargant 1967: 118).

The brother of a churchman who would become an Anglican bishop in Bangalore, India (Sargant 1967: 15), Sargant nevertheless held a reductionist view of religion. Starting from Pavlov's canine experiments, he observed that when they were stimulated transmarginally (i.e., beyond their normal reaction capabilities) the dogs exhibited an anomalous behavior in three stages. In the first, called equivalent, they reacted similarly to either weak or strong stimuli. In the second stage, called paradoxical, they reacted to the weak stimulus in a more meaningful way than to the strong one. In the third, ultra-paradoxical stage, the dogs' habitual responses were inverted. For example, reactions of sympathy to the researcher changed into hostility (Sargant 1957: 38–39).

Sargant was persuaded that Soviet and Chinese forms of brainwashing confirmed that "though men are not dogs, they should humbly try to remember how much they resemble dogs in their brain functions, and not boast themselves as demigods" (Sargant 1957: 239). By employing a wide range of transmarginal stimuli – from the rolling of drums to intense fear, from the obsessive repetition of jingles to some types of singing and dancing – a human being could be led, just like Pavlov's dogs, to the ultra-paradoxical stage where "people can be switched to arbitrary beliefs altogether opposed to those previously held" (Sargant 1957: 26).

The central argument in Sargant's work is that Communists did not invent brainwashing. At most, thanks to Pavlov they reached a better understanding of the process, which they adapted from preexisting religious revivalism and conversion processes. He wrote: "Anyone who wishes to investigate the technique of brainwashing and eliciting confessions as practiced behind the Iron Curtain (and on this side of it, too, in certain police stations where the spirit of the law is flouted) would do well to start with a study of eighteenth-century American revivalism from the 1730's onwards" (Sargant 1957: 148). In Sargant's estimation, the leading precursor of Communist Pavlovian techniques was John Wesley (1703–91), the founder of Methodism. Sargant made frequent, if uncomplimentary, parallels between Wesley's followers and Pavlov's dogs. The great English preacher was said to have been able to "disrupt previous patterns of behavior" and belief and instill new ones through "assaults on the brain," just as Pavlov did with his dogs (Sargant 1957: 98).

Nor did Sargant stop at Wesley. He also offered examples from the American preachers Jonathan Edwards (1703–58) and Charles Grandison Finney (1792–1875), as well as Ignatius of Loyola (1491–1556), the Catholic founder of the Jesuits (Sargant 1957: 131). Speaking of Jonathan Edwards, Sargant observed that "all the physiological mechanisms exploited by Pavlov in his animal experiments, short of glandular change by castration, seem, in fact, to have been exploited by Edwards or his successors" (Sargant 1957: 152).

Even the Apostle Paul's conversion as recorded in the New Testament, Sargant argued, might be explained through a Pavlovian scheme, with the Christian Ananias brainwashing the Jewish, and originally anti-Christian, Paul. "A state of transmarginal inhibition seems to have followed his [Paul's] acute stage of nervous excitement ... [and] increased his anxiety and suggestibility . ... Ananias came to relieve his nervous symptoms and his mental distress, at the same time implanting new beliefs" (Sargant 1957: 121).

Lest he be accused of anti-Christian prejudices, Sargant was quick to add that brainwashing was already at work in pre-Christian religions. Among Sargant's closest friends was Robert Graves (1895–1985), a British poet influential in the modern neopagan revival. Graves edited *Battle for the Mind*, giving it the literary form that made it a bestseller, and later Sargant's autobiography as well (Sargant 1967: 174). Graves also agreed to write a chapter of *Battle for the Mind*, entitled "Brain-Washing in Ancient Times" (Sargant 1957: 175–84). Its conclusion was that "almost identical physiological and psychological phenomena" are at work in "conversion techniques, equally in the most primitive and the more highly civilized cultures," and "they may be added as convincing proofs of the truth of [any] religious or philosophic beliefs." But since these contradictory beliefs cannot all be equally true, it follows that what they share is the "mechanistic principle" of conversion (Sargant 1957: 94; Sargant 1967: 175). Religions convert people to many different beliefs, but what they have in common is that they all convert through brainwashing.

On November 5, 1968, Sargant was invited to give the premiere annual public lecture of the British psychiatric world, the 43rd Maudsley Lecture, before the Royal Medico-Psychological Association. His topic was "The Physiology of Faith." In the lecture, published in 1971 as an introduction to the third edition of *Battle for the Mind* (Sargant 1971: 1–35), Sargant was unrepentant in defending his controversial 1957 work. He insisted that the Pavlovian model had been applied "at every time in man's long religious history" (Sargant 1971: 25), up until recently created religions such as Scientology (Sargant 1971: 19). Sargant denied that it was his purpose to destroy religion. On the contrary, he said, there is a need for religion and, in any case, brainwashing is omnipresent in social life.

Although all religions use brainwashing, Sargant maintained that to distinguish useful ones from those that are harmful, we ought to inspect the kind of conduct that each religion inspires – "what it results in and makes of the lives of those who come to believe in it" (Sargant 1971: 35). As Sargant had written in *Battle for the Mind*, "the proof of the pudding lies in the eating" (Sargant 1957: 118). Although Wesley treated his followers like Pavlovian dogs, he saved many Englishmen from drunkenness and political rebelliousness.

As to the future of religion, "it seems possible" concluded Sargant in 1968, "that modern tranquilizers, such as chlorpromazine, if given continuously, will diminish the average person's chances of acquiring sudden faith" (Sargant 1971: 31). For the time being, lobotomy was a possibility to reverse the consequences of religious brainwashing. Sargant reported that through lobotomy he had once persuaded a Salvation Army worker who was enthusiastic about the Holy Ghost to proclaim after the surgery that "[t]here is no Holy Ghost" (Sargant 1957: 89).

"Only Cults Brainwash": Margaret Thaler Singer

Sargant believed that all religions use brainwashing. In this respect, he made no substantial distinction between religions and cults. In the United States, however, a significant movement opposing cults developed in the late 1960s and became interested in brainwashing theories.

In 1993, I made a distinction between a sectarian countercult and a secular anticult movement, which has been widely adopted since (Introvigne 1993). The countercult movement started in the early nineteenth century, when Protestant and later Roman Catholic theologians systematically criticized what they considered to be heretical cults that departed from Christian orthodoxy. This movement continued into the twentieth century and is still present today. Countercultists were mostly interested in doctrines they identified as heretical, and wanted to bring cultists back to the orthodox Christian fold. They rarely asked governments to legislate against cults, but instead fought their battles through books, articles, and lectures.

The anticult movement, on the other hand, was created in North America by parents of young adults who, in the late 1960s and 1970s, had joined new religious movements as full-time members, renouncing secular careers. The missions of these movements, both coming from Asia (such as the Unification Church) and born in America (e.g., the Children of God), were successful among college students who were influenced by the hippie movement. They saw in the new religions an alternative to pursuing what some considered dull bourgeois careers.

Most parents had no quarrel with what mainline Christians regarded as unorthodox theologies. However, they strongly objected to the fact that their children had decided to drop out of college and serve as full-time missionaries. The anticult movement was thus born and had three important differences from the old religious countercult movement. First, it proclaimed not to be interested in creeds, only in deeds, and it defined a cult not on the basis of its theology but on the social harm it caused. Second, it only aimed at persuading the cultists to abandon the cult and go back to pursuing a normal career. It was not interested in converting them back to their parents' religion. Third, it tried to enroll the cooperation of governments and courts of law, which would not be open to theological criticism of heresies but might perhaps be persuaded by secular arguments.

An organization called Free Our Sons and Daughters from the Children of God (FREECOG) was founded in 1971–2 by the parents of some who had joined the Children of God. Parents of young adult members of controversial groups other than the Children of God, and professionals such as lawyers and psychologists, also joined the new anticult movement, creating the Citizen's Freedom Foundation (CFF). FREECOG and CFF later merged to become the Cult Awareness Network (CAN). Soon, it also started targeting human potential or neo-gnostic groups such as the Church of Scientology. At the same time, a number of anticult movements were created in Western Europe, including FAIR (Family, Action, Information, Rescue) in the United Kingdom in 1976, and ADFI (the Association pour la défense des valeurs familiales et de l'individu [Association for the defense of family values and individuals], later Association de défense des familles et de l'individu [Association for the defense of families and individuals]) in France in 1974, where several local ADFIs federated in a national UNADFI in 1982.

Psychologists brought to the anticult movement Sargant-style theories of brainwashing, but claimed that they did not apply to genuine or mainline religions. Only cults, they said, use brainwashing and, conversely, the use of brainwashing identifies a movement as a cult.

The anticult movement pursued its aims through three different tools. First, it launched a number of public awareness campaigns claiming that brainwashing was real and cults were a major threat. It managed to establish close relationships with several media personalities, who created a sinister image of the cults that persists to this day.

Second, the anticult movement lobbied US local and state legislators to introduce anti-brainwashing statutes and supported some well-publicized court actions in which former members who had left new religious movements claimed they had been brainwashed and sued for damages. Ultimately, constitutional concerns prevailed, and no anticult legislation was passed in any state. Some of the court cases were successful, while most were not.

Third, the anticultists supported a new practice called deprogramming, which had been created by Ted Patrick, a California state bureaucrat whose son had encountered the Children of God (now called The Family International). Patrick was among the founders of FREECOG and developed a technique involving the kidnapping of cultists and their detention in secluded facilities. Here, they were bombarded with negative information about their cult until they surrendered and deconverted. Other parents joined and deprogramming as a mirror image of brainwashing became a lucrative, if not always successful, profession (Shupe and Bromley 1980). Patrick insisted that the violence inherent in deprogramming was needed because the victims had previously been brainwashed (Patrick 1976). After some initial tolerance, the courts eventually disagreed. Some deprogrammers had to pay heavy damages, and some went to jail.

Anticultists became concerned about their potential liability in cases against the deprogrammers and decided to keep a lower profile. Some decided to abandon the pro-deprogramming CFF and to focus more on research, education, and propaganda. In 1979, these moderates eventually established the American Family Foundation (AFF), later renamed the International Cultic Studies Association (ICSA).

"Jolly" West – who, as mentioned earlier, had participated in CIA projects – and Margaret Thaler Singer (1921–2003) became leading figures in the anticult movement. West rarely testified in the courts on the matter of cults. His epidemiological theory of brainwashing, which considered the joining of cults to be a disease and an epidemic (West 1989), found only limited acceptance (Galanter 1990). The brainwashing theory applied to the cults by the anticult movement in the 1970s and 1980s is largely a construction of Singer. She was a clinical psychologist who had collaborated in the past with Schein and coauthored some articles with him (Strassman, Thaler, and Schein 1956; Singer and Schein 1958; Schein and Singer 1992). Singer was also an adjunct lecturer at the University of California, Berkeley from 1964 to 1991. She appeared in court as an expert witness testifying against the cults so often that, in a sense, she invented a new profession as a psychologist, almost full-time, in the service of anticult lawsuits and initiatives. Singer made frequent use of terms such as Schein's coercive persuasion and Lifton's thought reform, treating them as synonyms for brainwashing (Singer and Lalich 1995: 53, 381). Her theory of brainwashing was, however, largely original.

Singer suggested a framework of six conditions for brainwashing: "keep the person unaware that there is an agenda to control or change the person"; "control time and physical environment (contacts, information)"; "create a sense of powerlessness, fear, and dependency"; "suppress old behavior and attitudes"; "instill new behavior and attitudes"; and "put forth a closed system of logic" (Singer and Lalich, 1995: 64). She did not just claim that a cult is quantitatively different from other institutions committed to changing ideas and behavior – including the army, jails, and mainline religions – because it indoctrinates more intensely than others. She believed she had identified the brainwashing process used by the cults as something qualitatively different from the methods employed by legitimate institutions and not connected with the doctrines or the "content of the group" (Singer and Lalich 1995: 61).

Singer insisted that the marines, prisoner rehabilitation programs, and mainline religions practice a legitimate type of indoctrination, while the cults use brainwashing. An important difference, she insisted, is deceit. According to Singer, recruits to the marines or the Jesuits know exactly what sort of organization they are joining, while those who approach the cults are recruited by deception. "Marine recruiters do not pretend to be florists or recruiters for children's clubs. Nor do Jesuits go afield claiming they are 'just an international living group teaching breathing exercises to clear the mind of stress'" (Singer and Lalich 1995: 98–101).

Approaching potential converts without disclosing the movement's name or identity is something that has certainly been practiced by some new religious movements criticized as cults, but not by all, nor by the majority of them. In almost all cases where she testified in court, Singer quoted her research on the Unification Church, founded by the Korean self-styled messiah Sun Myung Moon (1920–2012). She could rightly state that at a certain point in its history, and in a specific location (Oakland, California), Moon's church was in fact enticing young people to attend its seminars without revealing the organizing group's identity. This practice was, however, restricted to a special subgroup of the Unification Church, the so-called Oakland Family. It was never generalized in Moon's organization and was comparatively short-lived (Barker 1984). Critics of Singer maintained that generalizing the Oakland Family's practices as if they were typical of the Unification Church everywhere, or of cults in general, was grossly unfair.

From the end of the 1970s and throughout the 1980s, Singer, together with sociologist Richard Ofshe (Ofshe and Singer 1986; Singer and Ofshe 1990) regularly cooperated with anticult organizations and attorneys, testifying in courts of law in the United States and elsewhere that brainwashing was a reality and a crime, and that cults were guilty of it. Although they tried to introduce some distinctions, Singer and Ofshe were often perceived as justifying deprogramming. This made their advocacy even more controversial, particularly after some deprogrammers were accused of resorting to drugs, physical violence, and even sexual abuse to deprogram their victims (Shupe and Darnell 2006).

The Cult Wars

From the end of the 1970s and throughout the 1980s, the outcome of the legal battles about cults in the United States looked uncertain. The lower court judges, especially in small town courts far from the large cities, were sympathetic to the parents' arguments. Sometimes, they even cooperated with the deprogrammers by entrusting into the custody of the parents, for periods of time, grown-up children who were ruled to be temporarily mentally incapacitated so that they could be deprogrammed without objection. But most of these decisions were overturned on appeal.

A brainwashing defense was also rejected in the sensational 1976 trial of heiress Patty Hearst, who had been kidnapped by the left-wing group Symbionese Liberation Army (SLA) in 1974. She had subsequently participated in bank robberies and other crimes perpetrated by the SLA. Singer and West stated that Hearst was not responsible for the crimes, as she had been brainwashed by the SLA. The brainwashing defense, however, was not accepted by the jury and Hearst was sentenced to thirty-five years in prison, later reduced to seven, then to twenty-two months by an act of President Jimmy Carter, until President Bill Clinton granted her a full pardon in 2001 (Richardson 2014).

In its well-known 1977 ruling, *Katz v. Superior Court*, a California Court of Appeals overturned an order that had granted temporary custody to parents of members of the Unification Church. In their decision, the Court of Appeals judges asked whether investigating if a conversion "was induced by faith or by coercive persuasion is ... not in turn investigating and questioning the validity of that faith," which is clearly prohibited under the US Constitution (Court of Appeals of California 1977). Coercive persuasion was Schein's terminology, although the judges used it in the sense that Singer had since given it. For all purposes, *Katz* put an end to temporary custody orders issued on behalf of deprogrammers. It also suggested that too often brainwashing theories functioned as no more than an attempt to use a pseudoscientific language to mask value judgments about unpopular beliefs.

In 1978, one year after *Katz*, the Peoples Temple homicides and suicides in Guyana created panic against cults all over the world, breathing new life into the anticult movement. In this new climate, deprogramming found fresh impetus. Some attorneys linked to the anticult movement pursued new strategies meant to induce former, deprogrammed members to claim damages for the brainwashing to which the cults had allegedly subjected them. For a number of reasons, the legal battle focused on the lawsuit of David Molko and Tracy Leal, two teenagers (by then of age) who had joined the San Francisco Unification Church despite their respective parents' strong opposition. Six months after joining, they had been successfully deprogrammed, to the extent that they brought a lawsuit against the Unification Church for damages they claimed to have suffered as a result of brainwashing.

In 1983 and 1986, two California courts rejected Molko and Leal's complaints. Two opposed camps on the issue of brainwashing existed at the time. On one side were the anticult associations, the deprogrammers, a small group of scholars who applied brainwashing theories to new religious movements, and several journalists. In the other camp were the new religious movements and their lawyers, NGOs that promoted religious freedom, some psychologists of religion, and most sociologists and historians who were busy defining the study of new religious movements as a new specialized academic field. In the latter group, the leading figures were psychologists Dick Anthony (1990, 1999, 2001) and H. Newton Malony (1931–2020), historian J. Gordon Melton, and sociologists James T. Richardson in the United States and Eileen Barker in Great Britain. In 1984, Barker had written what became the standard critique of brainwashing theories with respect to the Unification Church (Barker 1984). In a series of seminal articles, which would continue into the twenty-first century, Richardson dismantled the idea that cults can be distinguished from religions based on their alleged practice of brainwashing (Richardson 1978, 1993a, 1993c, 1996a, 2014, 2015).

The two camps faced each other in the courts, where they traded accusations of partisan advocacy. Those who supported the brainwashing theory were accused of covering up the illegal activities of the deprogrammers. They replied that the scholars of new religious movements were ignoring the similarly illegal activities of the cults, and were cult apologists paid by the new religions. For various reasons, the American Psychological Association (APA, not to be confused with the American Psychiatric Association that uses the same acronym) was caught in the eye of the storm. Similar problems also surfaced in the American Sociological Association (ASA), but these were less serious since, irrespective of the ASA, it was clear that an overwhelming majority of sociologists of religion did not agree with the brainwashing hypothesis and sided against Singer and Ofshe.

In 1983, during the *Molko* lawsuit, the APA accepted the proposal of forming a task force, known as DIMPAC (Deceptive and Indirect Methods of Persuasion and Control), for the purpose of assessing the scientific status of these theories. Margaret Singer, who headed the task force, chose the other members including Louis "Jolly" West and Michael D. Langone, a psychologist active in the AFF. The task force continued its work for several years. In the meantime, the *Molko* case reached the Supreme Court of California. According to a reconstruction of the events prepared in 1989 by the APA, "on 5 February 1987, during its winter meeting, the APA Board of Directors voted for APA to participate in the case [*Molko*] as an amicus" (American Psychological Association 1989: 1).

In the US legal system, an *amicus curiae* is an independent entity or individual that spontaneously submits to the court elements regarded as relevant to decide a case. On February 10, 1987, the APA and others filed an amicus brief in the *Molko* case. The brief stated that the theory Singer had labeled "coercive persuasion" was not "accepted in the scientific community," and that the corresponding methodology "has been repudiated by the scientific community." The brief went on to specify that the choice of labels, such as brainwashing, mental manipulation, or coercive persuasion (as used by Singer), was irrelevant because none of those theories could be considered to be scientific (American Psychological Association 1987a).

The filing of the brief provoked numerous protests. The community of psychologists and psychiatrists was divided on the subject: several clinical psychologists disagreed on the substance, while others denounced the method. How could the APA, after asking the DIMPAC task force to prepare a report on the subject, presumably to be accepted or rejected by the association, proceed to take an official position before having read and passed judgment on the report?

Several APA officials replied that there was no time to wait for the report of the DIMPAC committee if the APA wanted to have an impact on the ruling on the *Molko* case, which was expected soon and would presumably become an important precedent. The procedural argument found favor with many, while others were afraid that clinical psychologists would be persuaded by a campaign organized by Singer and West that suggested they resign from the APA en masse. For this reason, according to the APA's 1989 reconstruction of events, "the [APA] Board of Directors, in the spring of 1987, reconsidered its prior decision to participate in the brief and voted, narrowly, to withdraw" (American

Psychological Association 1989: 1). This meant, the Association said, that the "APA's decision to withdraw from the [*Molko*] case was based on procedural as opposed to substantive concerns. APA never rejected the brief [of February 10, 1987] on the grounds that it was inaccurate in substance" (American Psychological Association 1989: 2).

On March 24, 1987, the APA filed a motion in which it withdrew from the *Molko* case. In it, the APA stated that, "by this action, APA does not mean to suggest endorsement of any views opposed to those set forth in the amicus brief [of February 10, 1987]" (American Psychological Association 1987b: 2). In the meantime, the APA decided to reach some kind of conclusion about the DIMPAC task force, which had been functioning since 1983. At the end of 1986, the task force submitted to the Board of Social and Ethical Responsibility (BSERP), the APA board in charge of public policy, a draft of its report. Subsequently, Singer and others claimed that it was not a final draft. In actuality, according to BSERP, the draft had been filed as a "final draft of the report, minus the reference list" (Thomas 1986).

The DIMPAC report presented two main theses. The first was that cults are not religions. They should not be labeled new religions or new religious movements since the use of these terms "results in ... an attitude of deviance deamplification toward extremist cults, and a tendency to gloss over critical differences between cultic and non-cultic groups" (DIMPAC 1986: 13).

The second thesis answered the question regarding how it is possible to differentiate between cults and religions. Unlike a religion, the report claimed, a cult is

> a group or movement exhibiting a great or excessive devotion or dedication to some person, idea, or thing and employing unethically manipulative (i.e., deceptive and indirect) techniques of persuasion and control designed to advance the goals of the group's leaders, to the actual or possible detriment of members, their families, or the community (DIMPAC 1986: 14).

These techniques include "isolation from former friends and family, debilitation, use of special methods to heighten suggestibility and subservience, powerful group pressures, information management, suspension of individuality or critical judgment, promotion of total dependency on the group and fear of leaving it, etc." (DIMPAC 1986: 14). In short, "totalist cults ... are likely to exhibit three elements to varying degrees: (1) excessively zealous, unquestioning commitment by members to the identity and leadership of the group; (2) exploitative manipulation of members; and (3) harm or the danger of harm" (DIMPAC 1986: 14).

The BSERP found that the draft had sufficient information to warrant issuing a statement and forwarded it to two internal and two external auditors. The latter were Jeffrey D. Fisher, from the University of Connecticut, and Benjamin Beit-Hallahmi, from the University of Haifa, Israel. With the BSERP statement, the APA not only rejected the DIMPAC report; it directed that it could not be referred to as an APA report – which was rightly perceived by APA members as a strong indictment of the document's content.

In the "publicly distributed" version of the BSERP statement (Singer and Ofshe 1994: 31), the only attachments were the opinions of Fisher and Beit-Hallahmi, the two external auditors. In a later lawsuit however, the opinion of one of the internal auditors, American psychologist and academic Catherine Grady, was also filed. According to Grady, in the task force's estimation the coercive persuasion techniques used by new religious movements "are not defined and cannot be distinguished from methods used in advertising, elementary schools, main-line churches, AA [Alcoholics Anonymous], and Weight Watchers." Moreover, the references to "harm" in the DIMPAC report were extremely confused: "It's all unsubstantiated and unproved newspaper reports and unresolved court cases. It's not evidence" (Grady 1987: 1–2).

Fisher wrote that the report was "unscientific in tone, and biased in nature" and "sometimes . . . characterized by the use of deceptive, indirect techniques of persuasion and control – the very thing it is investigating." He also observed that, "At times, the reasoning seems flawed to the point of being almost ridiculous." Fisher added that the report's historical excursion on the cults "reads more like hysterical ramblings than a scientific task force report." On the DIMPAC task force's criticism of the use of the expression new religious movements and argument that the term cults should be retained, Fisher countered that "the reasoning becomes absolutely some of the most polemical, ridiculous reasoning I've ever seen anywhere, much less in the context of an A.P.A. technical report" (BSERP 1987: 2–3).

In his review of the report, Beit-Hallahmi asked,

> What exactly are deceptive and indirect techniques of persuasion and control? I don't think that psychologists know much about techniques of persuasion and control, either direct or indirect, either deceptive or honest. We just don't know, and we should admit it. Lacking psychological theory, the report resorts to sensationalism in the style of certain tabloids (BSERP 1987: 4).

He added that,

> psychotherapy as it is practiced most of the time (private practice) is likely to lead to immoral behavior. I have no sympathy for Rev. Moon, Rajneesh, or

> Scientology, but I think that psychologists will be doing the public a greater
> favor by cleaning their own act, before they pick on various strange religions
> (BSERP 1987: 5).

A scholar hostile to the cults, Beit-Hallahmi nevertheless offered a radical conclusion: "The term 'brainwashing' is not a recognized theoretical concept, and is just a sensationalist 'explanation' more suitable to 'cultists' and revival preachers. It should not be used by psychologists since it does not explain anything" (BSERP 1987: 5).

Although the DIMPAC report declared that the task force had succeeded in finding a secular test to distinguish between cults and religions, which was not based on their "professed beliefs" but on their "actual practices" of persuasion and control (DIMPAC 1986: 14–15), the APA reviewers disagreed. They suspected that, contrary to what the report stated, the task force first classified some groups as cults because it regarded their beliefs as so irrational that nobody would freely embrace them. Then they introduced "deceptive and indirect techniques of persuasion and control," that is, brainwashing, as an explanation for otherwise inexplicable conversions.

On May 11, 1987, as a result of the reviewers' opinions, the BSERP, speaking on behalf of the APA, issued a Memorandum evaluating what it called the "task force's final report." The BSERP rejected the DIMPAC report on the grounds that it "lacks the scientific rigor and evenhanded critical approach necessary for APA imprimatur" (BSERP 1987: 1). In subsequent years, this Memorandum became the object of extensive controversy as Singer did not accept the APA verdict. She remained convinced that it was the result of a sinister "Conspiracy" (she always capitalized the word) plotted by APA's top management and leading international scholars of new religious movements who acted together "fraudulently, intentionally, falsely, and/or in reckless disregard for the truth, with intent to deceive and in furtherance of the Conspiracy" (Singer and Ofshe 1994: 30).

Singer and her colleague Ofshe did not stop at verbal accusations. They filed a complaint in the US District Court, Southern District of New York, against APA, ASA, and several individual scholars, accusing them of forming a racket and, as such, of being subject to anti-racketeering statutes that had originally been conceived to pursue organized crime. On August 9, 1993, the Court ruled that anti-racketeering laws "can have no role in sanctioning conduct motivated by academic and legal differences" (United States District Court for the Southern District of New York 1993). After losing in federal court, Singer turned to the laws of the State of California, producing what she believed was solid evidence of the Conspiracy. But she lost again. On June 17, 1994, Judge James R. Lambden ruled that "plaintiffs have not presented sufficient evidence to establish any reasonable probability of success on any cause of action" (Superior Court of the State of California in and for the County of Alameda 1994: 1).

In the 1990s lawsuits, Singer took it for granted that the 1987 BSERP Memorandum constituted "a rejection of the scientific validity of [her] theory of coercive persuasion" and was even described by the APA as such (Singer and Ofshe 1994: 31). Later, however, some of Singer's supporters focused on the Memorandum's note in its fourth paragraph that "after much consideration, BSERP does not believe that we have sufficient information available to guide us in taking a position on this issue" (BSERP 1987: 1). Contrary to Singer's opinion, they argued that the Memorandum was not, in fact, a rejection of her theory of brainwashing, which had neither been accepted nor rejected by the BSERP.

But what was "this issue" on which the APA refused to "take a position"? It could not be the DIMPAC report, because the Memorandum did take a clear position on it. Nor could it be the subject matter of the DIMPAC report, that is, the brainwashing theory as presented by Singer and the anticult movement, because that theory was comprehensively illustrated in the report. It seems safe to conclude that the intent of the 1987 Memorandum was to argue that Singer's anticult brainwashing theory lacked scientific rigor, while not evaluating which different theories of persuasion may be acceptable or not – a much broader question on which understandably the Memorandum did not wish to take a position (see Introvigne 2014b).

Brainwashing in American Courts: From *Molko* to *Fishman*

We now return to the *Molko* Unification Church lawsuit. In 1988, Judge Stanley Mosk (1912–2001) of the California Supreme Court issued a ruling that over-turned the lower courts' judgment on the admissibility of Singer's and others' testimony on brainwashing theories. Judge Mosk held that, the *Katz* decision notwithstanding, it was constitutionally admissible to ascertain whether or not a group practices brainwashing. The *Molko* ruling did not consider the latest APA developments, and was supported by two arguments. First, Judge Mosk held that brainwashing theory had its supporters within academia, although it remained quite controversial. "Some commentators," he wrote, "conclude that certain religious groups use brainwashing techniques to recruit and control members. ... To the contrary, other authorities believe brainwashing either does not exist at all ... or is effective only when combined with physical abuse or physical restraint" (Supreme Court of the State of California 1988: 54).

Second, the judge asked the question whether accepting brainwashing theories would imply allowing into the case a distinction between good and bad religion, which was not allowed by the US Constitution. His answer was that considering whether a religious group had used deception, by attracting potential converts without telling them which movement had approached them, did not involve any judgment on theology. Mosk acknowledged that, from a structural point of view, the coercive influence to which participants to Unification Church sponsored seminars were exposed was no different from what novices underwent in a Catholic convent. But the differentiating factor, he said, was deceit: in the Oakland Family – the branch of the Unification Church that Molko and Leal had joined – those who attended workshops did not know, at least in the first few days that are crucial to decision-making, what organization they had been asked to join.

Catholic religious orders, the judge said, use the same coercive influence but do not deceive novices by hiding the name of the order. "It is one thing when a person knowingly and voluntarily submits to a process involving coercive influence, as a novice does on entering a monastery or a seminary . . . . But it is quite another when a person is subjected to coercive persuasion without his knowledge or consent" (Supreme Court of the State of California 1988: 60). Judge Mosk did not conclude that coercive influence, that is, brainwashing, was illegal per se. He said it was only illegal when it was accompanied by deceit.

Although the *Molko* lawsuit was later resolved in an out-of-court settlement, controversies continued. Singer and her critics crossed swords again in 1988 in the *Kropinsky* v. *World Plan Executive Council* case, when the Federal Court of Appeals for the District of Columbia unanimously overturned a lower court decision that had admitted her testimony about brainwashing in a case involving Transcendental Meditation. According to the Court of Appeals, the plaintiff "failed to provide any evidence that Dr. Singer's particular theory, namely that techniques of thought reform may be effective in the absence of physical threats or coercion, has a significant following in the scientific community, let alone general acceptance" (United States Court of Appeals, District of Columbia Circuit 1988).

Singer responded by starting what some of her critics nicknamed her "manual wars." What was in the mainline scientific manuals, she claimed, was not partisan advocacy but accepted science. The short entry in the diagnostic manual of the American Psychiatric Association DSM-III (American Psychiatric Association 1980: 260) about brainwashing, said to have been practiced on "the captives of terrorists or cultists," she claimed, had been written by herself. Singer's critics responded that, although the DSM-III manual was indeed an authoritative text, placing a short entry there did not in itself constitute sufficient proof that a controversial theory had found general acceptance (Richardson 1993b). In fact, in 1994, the DSM-IV that replaced DSM-III eliminated the reference to cultists in its coverage of unspecified dissociation disorders, although it retained the expression brainwashing, without defining it, and associated the practice with being a prisoner in a scenario of physical segregation (American Psychiatric Association 1994: 490). For several years, however, the DSM-III reference continued to be quoted to support the claim that brainwashing was part of mainline science (Anthony 1999: 436).

All of this became less relevant after the decisive battle between the two camps took place in the US District Court for the Northern District of California in 1990, in the *United States* v. *Fishman* case. Steven Fishman was a professional troublemaker, who attended the stockholders' meetings of large corporations for the purpose of suing the management with the support of other minority stockholders. He then signed settlements and pocketed the money paid by the corporations, leaving the other stockholders who had trusted him empty-handed. In a lawsuit brought against him for fraud, Fishman claimed in his defense that at the time he was temporarily incapable of understanding or forming sound judgments because he had been a member of the Church of Scientology since 1979 and, as such, had been subjected to brainwashing.

The case was not easy for Singer and Ofshe, who served as expert witnesses for Fishman's defense. In addition to Scientology not being part of the case, and having nothing to do with Fishman's fraudulent activities, the prosecutor easily showed that the defendant had been guilty of similar practices even before being introduced to Scientology. Notwithstanding this, Fishman's defense insisted on calling Singer and Ofshe to the stand.

On April 13, 1990, Judge D. Lowell Jensen ruled on the issue. He pointed out that, unlike the earlier *Kropinsky* case, here it was possible to review hundreds of academic documents on brainwashing. Unlike Judge Mosk in the *Molko* ruling, Jensen had a large file on his desk about the APA's position on the DIMPAC task force. He largely relied on the expert opinions rendered for the prosecution by Dick Anthony and psychiatrist Perry London (1931–92). Jensen stated that brainwashing theory as Singer presented it first emerged with journalist and CIA operative Edward Hunter and did not concur with the thought reform theory put forth by Lifton and Schein. Although Singer and Ofshe argued that they were faithfully applying Lifton and Schein's theories to the matter of cults, the judge noted that their claim "has met with resistance from members of the scientific community." Even though some of Singer's positions on brainwashing had been included in respected psychiatric manuals, "a more significant barometer of prevailing views within the scientific community is provided by professional organizations such as the American Psychological Association" (United States District Court for the Northern District of California 1990: 12–13).

Judge Jensen retraced the APA's intervention, stating that "the APA considered the scientific merit of the Singer–Ofshe position on coercive persuasion in the mid-1980s," by setting up the DIMPAC task force. It also "publicly endorsed a position on coercive persuasion contrary to Dr. Singer's'" by submitting a brief in the *Molko* case in which it was argued that the theory of brainwashing as applied to "cults [...] did not represent a meaningful scientific concept." It is true, Judge Jensen argued, that the APA subsequently withdrew its signature on this brief, but "in truth the withdrawal occurred for procedural and not substantive reasons," as confirmed by the fact that soon thereafter the APA "rejected the Singer task force report on coercive persuasion." The judge recalled that similar events had transpired in the ASA. Therefore, the documents "establish that the scientific community has resisted the Singer–Ofshe thesis applying coercive persuasions to religious cults." Jensen added that even Lifton, a scholar who had no sympathy for the cults, had expressed reservations about the Singer–Ofshe model (United States District Court for the Northern District of California 1990: 14).

To serve as the foundation for a legal decision, a scientific theory should find general acceptance in the academic community. In the case of brainwashing, Jensen said, "the Singer–Ofshe thesis lacks the imprimatur of the APA and the ASA . . . . Theories regarding the coercive persuasion practiced by religious cults are not sufficiently established to be admitted as evidence in federal courts of law" (United States District Court for the Northern District of California 1990: 14).

Three important conclusions were reached in the *Fishman* ruling. The first was that the APA did not simply refuse to approve the DIMPAC task force report; in 1987, it expressed disapproval of DIMPAC and Singer's theory of brainwashing more generally. Second, the size of the minority of scholars supporting brainwashing theory was too small to argue that there were two competing positions in academia. Rather, *Fishman* confirmed that there was a large, although not unanimous, consensus among scholars that brainwashing theories belonged to pseudoscience. Third, expert testimony on brainwashing should be excluded in cult cases. With this, *Fishman* established a precedent that continues to be followed in most cases in the United States to the present day (although the situation may be different in other countries).

Perhaps Jensen exaggerated Lifton's reservations about Singer's theories. Although he was aware that Singer's theory was different from his model of thought reform, Lifton repeatedly endorsed the anticult movement while resisting direct involvement in court cases. In 1995, Lifton wrote a three-page preface to Singer's popular book *Cults in Our Midst*, cowritten with Janja Lalich, which began by stating that "Margaret Thaler Singer stands alone in her extraordinary knowledge of the psychology of cults," although he also noted that "one person's cult, of course, is another's religion" and that any generalization was dangerous (Lifton 1995: xi–xiii).

Undoubtedly, the fact that Lifton agreed to write the preface was an important political achievement for Singer. In 2001, Lifton and I debated the issue of cults at a conference organized by the Axel and Margaret Ax:son Johnson Foundation in Sweden (Almqvist and Wallrup 2005). Lifton made it abundantly clear that he regarded cults as part of a harmful constellation of conservative, authoritarian forces using thought reform to limit the human capability for autonomous thinking. He included in this galaxy the US Republican Party of then-President George W. Bush. In 2017, Lifton would gladly join a group of psychiatrists in arguing that Donald Trump's mental state made him unfit to continue to serve as president (Lee 2017); and in 2019, he would compare the Trump movement with cults such as Aum Shinrikyo (Lifton 2019).

As much as he despised what he regarded as different incarnations of totalism, Lifton's libertarian ideas also made him cautious in approving anticult legislation and lawsuits. He saw the dangers for religious liberty, as well as the risks that a primitive, simplistic idea of brainwashing – of which he had never approved – would prevail. For him, freedom from religionists and politicians who continuously try to manipulate us should be achieved through culture and education.

After *Fishman*, it became more difficult for Margaret Singer and other anticult advocates to be accepted in US federal courts as expert witnesses on brainwashing, and this eventually created problems for them in state courts as well (Ginsburg and Richardson 1998). Deprogrammers found still less tolerance, even in local courts. The *Fishman* ruling did not spell the definitive end of the use of anticult brainwashing theories in US courts. However, a chain of events had been set in motion that would eventually lead to the end of deprogramming in the United States and the demise of CAN.

In 1995, deprogrammer Rick Ross was involved in a civil trial after he had unsuccessfully tried to deprogram Jason Scott, a member of the United Pentecostal Church, a five-million strong Christian denomination few would regard as either a cult or a new religious movement. Scott was supported by lawyers and detectives from the Church of Scientology, who demonstrated that his mother was referred to Ross by CAN. The latter was sentenced to pay millions of dollars in damages (United States Court of Appeals for the Ninth Circuit 1998) and went bankrupt. CAN's name and assets were purchased by a Scientology-related group, which allowed sociologist Anson D. Shupe (1948–2015) and his team free access to the CAN archives. They concluded that CAN's practice of referring the parents of cult members to deprogrammers was not an occasional but rather a habitual occurrence. In return for the referrals, the deprogrammers kicked back to CAN hefty (and probably illegal) commissions (Shupe and Darnell 2006).

Have Brainwashing Theory, Will Travel: US Experts Abroad

While Singer and others were prevented by *Fishman* from testifying about brainwashing in most American cult cases, they could still do so abroad. In the 1970s, an anticult movement had emerged in Europe, Canada, Australia–New Zealand, and in some South American countries in close contact with US organizations. US deprogrammers also started operating abroad (Shupe and Bromley 1994). By the 1980s, most claimed they were now using exit counseling or intervention, nonviolent processes that did not include kidnapping or detention, although some were accused of having changed their techniques in name only. Having experienced problems with deprogramming, the British anticult organization FAIR changed its name from "Family, Action, Information, Rescue" to "Family Action, Information, Resource" (and later to The Family Survival Trust). The word "rescue" was too easily associated with deprogramming.

The ambiguity of terminology was clearly demonstrated by the 1999 novel and movie *Holy Smoke!* by New Zealand screenwriters and directors Anna and Jane Campion (Campion and Campion 1999). An ambiguous sexual relation develops between the deprogrammer (played by Harvey Keitel) and the young female devotee of an Indian guru (portrayed by Kate Winslet) he tries to deprogram. What we see is a classical deprogramming; the girl is clearly told she is not free to leave the Australian farm where she has been confined, yet the man styles himself as an "exit counselor" (Introvigne 1999).

Although some countries made financial contributions to anticult organizations, the interest of governments outside the United States in campaigns or legislation against cults was initially not high. Italy was a special case, because of its century-old tradition of statutes on "*plagio.*" The word came from the Latin *plagium*, which in Roman times indicated two different crimes: appropriating somebody else's literary or artistic creations (hence the English word plagiarism) and appropriating free will and freedom by reducing into slavery a Roman citizen who was not legally a slave. In the second meaning, *plagio* came to indicate "reduction to slavery." In 1930 the Fascist regime codified it as a crime not only of physical, but also of mental enslavement. Something similar to brainwashing had thus been introduced into the Italian Criminal Code twenty years before the word brainwashing was invented by Hunter. The provision was used very rarely. Although it remained in the Criminal Code for fifty-one years, no conviction was based on it until 1968 (Usai 1996).

In 1964, the law on *plagio* was used to prosecute Aldo Braibanti (1922–2014), a gay Communist poet. The father of a young man who had decided to live with him accused Braibanti of having brainwashed his heterosexual son into homosexuality. Based on the statute on *plagio*, Braibanti was arrested, prosecuted, and sentenced to a jail term of nine years in 1968. The sentence was confirmed up to the Court of Cassation, notwithstanding a national campaign led by prominent intellectuals, who denounced both the decisions against Braibanti as homophobic and the *plagio* statute as a dangerous Fascist residue the Constitutional Court should eliminate (Moravia et al. 1969).

Braibanti's case never reached the Constitutional Court, however. The poet was liberated after two years in jail, thanks to a law that granted sentence reductions to those who had valiantly fought against the Fascist regime in the Italian Resistance, as he had done. The Braibanti decision led prosecutors to start a handful of other *plagio* cases in the 1970s. No convictions were obtained, however.

Among those prosecuted for *plagio* was Father Emilio Grasso, a popular Catholic priest from Rome who in 1978 was accused by parents of having brainwashed their sons and daughters into dropping out of college to serve as full-time lay missionaries for his movement, Redemptor Hominis. Rather than making a decision – unlike in the Braibanti case, and perhaps because Catholic priests were at that time more popular in Italy than gay poets – the judges in Rome requested a preliminary ruling from the Constitutional Court. They asked the Constitutional judges to determine whether the statute on *plagio*, which dated to 1930, was compatible with the new democratic Constitution of 1947. On June 8, 1981, the Constitutional Court decided that it was not. The justices stated that the *plagio* statute was a "bomb" hidden in the Italian legal system, "ready to explode" at any time against members of unpopular minorities. Noting that the scientific community had not established criteria distinguishing resistible and irresistible persuasion, the Court concluded that some

> situations of psychological dependency . . . can reach high degrees of intensity even for long periods, including in a love relationship, a relationship between priest and believer, teacher and pupil, physician and patient . . . But in practice, it is extremely difficult, if not impossible, to distinguish, in all these cases, a licit psychological persuasion from an allegedly illegal psychological manipulation, and to differentiate between them for legal purposes. No firm criteria exist for separating and defining the two activities, nor can a precise boundary between the two be traced
>
> (Corte Costituzionale 1981: 831–33).

During the cult wars and beyond, anticultists in Italy repeatedly tried to reintroduce provisions against *plagio* or brainwashing, but this proved impossible because of the binding nature of Constitutional Court precedents (Introvigne 2014a).

In Europe in general, anticultism was revitalized after the homicides and suicides perpetrated by the Order of the Solar Temple – a new religious movement based on a mixture of esoteric ideas and apocalyptic expectations – in Switzerland, France, and Canada, in 1994, 1995, and 1997, respectively. Several of those who died in the Solar Temple tragedy were wealthy professionals, which contrasted with the popular image of cults finding their followers mostly among marginal or poor segments of the population. This led both the media and authorities to suspect brainwashing (Introvigne and Mayer 2002).

In the wake of the Solar Temple incidents, parliamentary or administrative committees were appointed in many Western European countries (with the significant exception of Great Britain) that produced reports about cults or about specific groups. In some countries, the reports called for the appointment of anticult agencies, new bills, or amendments to existing laws that would make brainwashing a crime. Perhaps the most active anticult governmental agency is MILS, the Inter-Ministerial Mission for Combating Cults, which was created in France (later renamed MIVILUDES, Inter-Ministerial Mission for the Vigilance and Fight against Cultic Deviations).

In a study I coauthored with James T. Richardson, we reviewed the reports published between 1996 and 2000 (Richardson and Introvigne 2001), distinguishing between what we called Type I and Type II documents. Type I documents (Assemblée Nationale 1996; Chambre des Représentants de Belgique 1997; Groupe d'experts genevois 1997; Commission pénale sur les dérives sectaires 1999) were all published in French, in France, Belgium, and the French-speaking part of Switzerland, adopting the Singer-style model of brainwashing and calling for new legislation. Type II reports, including a Dutch report (Witteveen 1984) and a long document approved in Germany (Deutscher Bundestag 1998), considered the scholarly criticism of the anticult brainwashing model and were more nuanced in their conclusions.

In the end, Belgium did not legislate on brainwashing, but in 1998 created an administrative task force and an information center to combat cults. In 2001, France introduced a new provision in the Criminal Code (article 223–15-2), punishing with a jail penalty of up to three years those who use techniques creating a state of "physical or psychological subjection." Spain, which had not created a commission to study the issue of brainwashing, amended article 515 of its Criminal Code in 1995, declaring illegal associations that use "techniques to change or control the personality" of their members and threatening their leaders with a three-year jail sentence (Motilla 1999: 325–40).

These laws were mostly enforced against small, local cults in France (Palmer 2011) and elsewhere. The larger groups, including Scientology, successfully resisted prosecution based on concepts such as psychological subjection, which were difficult to prove in court against the objections of skilled defense lawyers and expert witnesses.

Margaret Singer continued to serve as an expert witness in several European cases. I was on the opposite side of the then-aging American psychologist in two cases in the 1990s, in France and Switzerland, respectively. Her side lost both cases. In France, she was gradually replaced as the leading anticult expert witness in the main court cases where cults were accused of brainwashing by French psychiatrist Jean-Marie Abgrall, who championed Singer's theories while presenting them in psychoanalytic jargon (Abgrall 1996; Anthony 1999).

European supporters of the theory that cults used brainwashing also relied on a handful of North American scholars who lectured in support of campaigns against Scientology and other new religious movements (Richardson 1996b). Janja Lalich, who had coauthored the classic *Cults in Our Midst* with Singer and based her writings on what she described as her personal experience in a political cult, the Marxist-Leninist Democratic Workers Party, has continued the Singer tradition into the twenty-first century. In the subsequent generation of anticultists, a similar role is played by South African-born Alexandra Stein, a social psychologist based in England (Stein 2016). Like Lalich, she also encountered brainwashing theories when reflecting on her time in what she also called a political cult, the Minneapolis Maoist group known as The O (Stein 2002). Self-styled cult experts who had been active in deprogramming, such as Steven Hassan and Rick Ross, also lecture internationally and keep alive Singer's model. As late as 2020, Hassan was still promoting the classic theory of brainwashing and even Singer's idea that it had been marginalized in academia through a conspiracy of scholars who were paid by the cults (Hassan 2020: 8).

In his history of the academic study of new religious movements, W. Michael Ashcraft noted that a handful of scholars seceded from the majority of their colleagues to create a new discipline they called cultic studies. This branch accepts the distinction between religions and cults and identifies cults by their use of heavy psychological manipulation techniques, for which some scholars retain the word brainwashing. As Ashcraft observed, cultic studies was never accepted as mainstream scholarship. It continued as "a project shared by a small cadre of committed scholars" but not endorsed by "the larger academic community, nationally and internationally" (Ashcraft 2018: 9).

The two main exponents of cultic studies realized that brainwashing theory, as originally formulated by Singer, could not survive decades of heavy scholarly criticism. Brainwashing, they believed, should be presented differently. Canadian sociologist Stephen A. Kent noted that most critics of anticult theories, and perhaps L. Ron Hubbard when he published *Brain-Washing*, denied that brainwashing was possible in the absence of extreme physical coercion yet accepted that it would be possible to overcome free will by using confinement or torture (Kent 2000: 10). Kent argued that new religious movements scholars wrongly believe that imprisonment and torture, while practiced by thought reformers in Maoist China, are not present in the cults. He insisted that institutions for reeducating "sinful" members – such as the Rehabilitation Project Force in the Church of Scientology or the Victor Camps created by The Family International (formerly Children of God) to reform rebellious teenagers – were brainwashing facilities where victims were "subjected to veritable forms of torture" (Kent 2000: 14). The argument has failed to convince scholars of new religious movements, who have objected that Kent has mostly relied on partisan accounts by apostates (Melton 2018), but the Canadian scholar has become a popular lecturer in the international anticult circuit.

Another scholar who proposed a somewhat revised theory of brainwashing was American sociologist Benjamin Zablocki (1941–2020). He presented brainwashing as "a technique for *retaining* members, not for *obtaining* members" (Zablocki 1997, 1998: 218). His analysis of brainwashing as a "maximization of exit costs" was different from Kent's, because Zablocki considered the search for physical coercion a "false path" (Zablocki 1998: 231). He believed there was no need for physical force to lead cult members to believe that, should they leave the group, they would incur intolerable exit costs. Exiting the movement, they were told, might prejudice their eternal salvation and their possibility of continuing a normal life. Zablocki also criticized Singer, insisting that brainwashing did not explain why some joined a cult, only why they did not leave. He also argued that brainwashing worked only in a limited number of cases (Zablocki 1998: 229).

Critics have objected that exit costs are maximized in a large number of legitimate social institutions, including the family and mainline religions (Bromley 1998: 250–71). Indeed, using Zablocki's model it is not easy to distinguish between religion and cults, and it has met with limited success even within the anticult milieu. On the other hand, because of his moderate approach Zablocki became one of the participants who represented the cultic studies side in a dialogue with mainline new religious movements scholars. The dialogue aimed, if not at resolving differences, at least at avoiding the name-calling and lawsuits typical of the cult wars years. In the twenty-first century, thanks to the efforts of Eileen Barker, Michael Langone, and others, this dialogue has increasingly involved both proponents of brainwashing theories and their critics.

Anticultists in South Korea and Japan have remained outside of these dialogues. They stuck to a crude brainwashing theory and to deprogramming, which in these countries was mostly practiced by conservative Protestant ministers. They combined a countercult theological criticism of heresies with anticult brainwashing theories, an approach that had been advocated earlier in Europe by German Lutheran pastor Friedrich-Wilhelm Haack (1935–91), who coined the word soulwashing (*seelenwäsche*) (Haack 1979: 116). In Japan, deprogramming was not ended by the law courts (Fautré 2012) until the seminal decision of the Tokyo High Court in the case of Unification Church member Goto Toru in 2014, who was detained against his will for more than twelve years, and then confirmed by the Supreme Court in 2015 (Fautré 2015).

In South Korea, deprogramming continues to this day, particularly against the Christian new religious movement, *Shincheonji*. This is despite massive street demonstrations in 2018 after a female member of that group, Gu Ji-In (1992–2018), was strangled to death by her father while she tried to escape deprogrammers (Fautré 2020). South Korean deprogrammers even produced propaganda videos proposing a unique mix of Singer-style brainwashing theories and Christian criticism of "unbiblical heresies" (Di Marzio 2020).

In Japan (Fautré 2021) and South Korea (Introvigne 2020), brainwashing arguments continue to be used to award damages to some former members of groups labeled as cults. Local courts, however, adopted the model of the *Molko* decision. They only ruled in favor of the ex-members when they found either that they had been recruited without having initially being told which groups they were asked to join or were induced to donate money under false pretenses. In cases where they believed deceit was not proved, the courts concluded there had been no brainwashing and refused to award damages (Introvigne 2020).

Russia and China are special cases. In post-Soviet Russia, anticult activities were initially promoted by the Russian Orthodox Church (ROC), based on theological criticism against unwelcome competitors in a religious market that was just opening after decades of state-enforced atheism. The ROC's criticism of the heretics, however, was largely perceived as old-fashioned and unpersuasive. It failed to effectively contain the growth of new religions coming from both Asia and the United States.

In 1992, Alexander Dvorkin, a Russian who had become an American citizen, returned to Moscow from the United States, where he had spent fifteen years, converted to Orthodox Christianity and obtained college degrees in

Theology and Medieval Studies. In the United States, Dvorkin had been exposed to the anticult theories of brainwashing. Upon his return to Russia, he sought employment with the ROC which quickly came to see in him a man of providence, sent to modernize the dusty anticultism of the church and make it palatable to the secular authorities through the theory of brainwashing (Shterin and Richardson 2000). Just one year after he had arrived in Russia, he became the head of the newly established countercult branch of the ROC, the Saint Irenaeus of Lyon Information and Consultation Center, and a professor of Cultic Studies at the ROC University of Saint Tikhon (Human Rights Without Frontiers Correspondent in Russia 2012).

While firmly grounded in Russian Orthodox theology, Dvorkin's narrative about the danger of the cults aimed to persuade the officially secular (but deeply indebted to the ROC for electoral and political support) Russian politicians that anticult action should be taken. After 9/11, and several terrorist attacks by Islamic fundamentalists on Russian soil, the Russian Parliament passed increasingly severe laws on "religious extremism." Dvorkin managed to persuade the authorities that brainwashing, typically used by the cults, was one of the features of extremism, although not the only one.

In 2009, Dvorkin was appointed head of the government's Council of Religious Experts with a crucial role in designating which groups should be regarded as extremist – inter alia because they used brainwashing – and banned. Although he occasionally embarrassed both the government and the ROC for his violent language and attacks against mainline Hinduism and Islam, which had caused international political problems for Russia, he managed to have Jehovah's Witnesses banned in Russia in 2017 and continued to target other new religious movements such as Scientology (USCIRF 2020: 3–5).

While the main financial support for European anticultism had traditionally come from the French government (Duval 2012), Russia started to court anticult organizations in various countries and promoted Dvorkin as an international expert on brainwashing and cults. In 2009, Dvorkin was elected vice president of the European Federation of Research and Information Centers on Sectarianism (FECRIS), a position he maintained until 2021. None of the more secular European anticult leaders –some of them self-styled atheists – object to having a ROC employee in this position. In 2020, the United States Commission on International Religious Freedom, a bipartisan commission of the US federal government, identified both Dvorkin and FECRIS among the main threats to the global cause of religious liberty, denouncing them for their promotion of "pseudo-scientific concepts like 'brainwashing' and 'mind control'" (USCIRF 2020: 3).

Dvorkin and other supporters of Singer-style brainwashing theories, including American deprogrammer Rick Ross, also visited China. There, in 1999, a new nationwide campaign had been launched to eradicate cults after the start of the conflict between the authorities and Falun Gong, the qigong new religion that had grown rapidly in the 1990s (Edelman and Richardson 2005). Eventually, China organized the largest and most-funded anticult association in the world. In its repression of religious movements it labeled as *xie jiao*, it started using the Western rhetoric of brainwashing.

While attending a conference with Chinese anticultists and law enforcement officers working full-time against the cults (*KKNews* 2017), I was surprised to learn that none of them was aware of the fact that the word brainwashing had originally been coined within the context of Western anti-Chinese and anti-Communist propaganda. On the other hand, as noted by the Chinese scholar Wu Junqing, contemporary Chinese anticultists did not need Western sources to use the rhetoric of brainwashing against the cults. They simply secularized the traditional Chinese theme of *xie jiao*, which lured victims through black magic (Wu 2017: 155–58). "We need not suppose that today's functionaries read ... imperial anecdotes" about black magic and *xie jiao*, Wu argued. "Popular novels and films" depicting the sinister techniques used by cults in Imperial China would be enough for the purpose (Wu 2017: 157).

Believing in cultic brainwashing, both Russians and the Chinese also accept the use of deprogramming. In these countries deprogramming is practiced in state-sponsored facilities and jails, rather than as a private activity, and cultists are sentenced to spend time there by court decisions or administrative orders (Richardson 2011). In Russia, deprogramming facilities are managed by the ROC and the Dvorkin group (Human Rights Without Frontiers Correspondent in Russia 2012: 279–80). In China, deprogramming is practiced in coercive educational facilities, such as the so-called transformation through education camps, in dedicated homes, and in jails (Cai 2021).

When in 2021 the BBC broadcast a report on the Xinjiang camps, giving voice to several women who had been reeducated for their alleged Islamic radical leanings, it told a tale very much reminiscent of the Maoist thought reform studied by Lifton. The women reported that, besides long hours of propaganda lessons, they were submitted to sleep and food deprivation and to a system of punishment and rewards based on their progress on the deradicalization path. They were also forced to take pills and injections that were introduced to them as vaccinations but left the women numb and confused, as if they were actually mind-altering drugs (Hill, Campanale, and Gunter 2021).

5 Conclusion: Old Wine in New Bottles

In the second half of the 1990s, James T. Richardson, who played an important role in criticizing brainwashing theories as applied to new religious movements, joined forces with legal scholar Gerald P. Ginsburg and others to systematically survey all American court cases where the word brainwashing appeared. Richardson and his colleagues continued the surveys into the twenty-first century, and published a summary of their research in 2015 (Reichert, Richardson, and Thomas 2015). They found that after *Fishman*, the use of brainwashing arguments in legal cases involving new religious movements had greatly decreased, although there were attempts to reintroduce them from time to time. Nevertheless, this did not mean that brainwashing had disappeared from American courts.

Richardson and his coauthors found that the words brainwashing, mind control, and cult had emerged between the *Fishman* decision of 1990 and 2014 in more than 900 American court cases, most of them not involving new religious movements. Brainwashing by a variety of sources (including teachers, pastors, therapists, and even the US government) was used, although rarely with success, as a defense in criminal cases, just as had happened in *Fishman* and in the earlier Patty Hearst case.

Much more successful was the idea, used in custody litigation, that one divorced parent had brainwashed children into hating their other parent. This was called parental alienation syndrome (PAS), a theory put forward by American child psychiatrist Richard A. Gardner (1931–2003), who explicitly based it on brainwashing (Gardner 1992). Answering his critics in an article published posthumously, he wrote that, "It is true that I do focus on the brainwashing parent, but I do not agree that such focus is 'overly simplistic.' The fact is that when there is PAS, the primary etiological factor is the brainwashing parent. And when there is no brainwashing parent, there is no PAS" (Gardner 2004: 614).

Gardner's theory was not unanimously accepted. In a remake of the 1987 DIMPAC case involving Singer's brainwashing theory, a Presidential Task Force of the APA concluded in 1996 that "there are no data to support the phenomenon called parental alienation syndrome" (American Psychological Association 1996, 40). Criticism came both from psychologists and legal scholars, including San Diego State University's Janet R. Johnston (Kelly and Johnston 2001; Johnston and Kelly 2004), and from critics of brainwashing theories such as Richardson (Richardson et al. 1995; Reichert, Richardson, and Thomas 2015: 13; Thomas and Richardson 2015). However, PAS continues to be used as an argument in divorce and custody cases, not only in the United

States; and the heated discussion about Gardner's theories keeps alive an international controversy on brainwashing.

Coercive control – defined as intimidation, surveillance, and isolation within a context of domestic abuse or stalking – also remains controversial. California and Hawaii, England and Wales, and Tasmania and Queensland in Australia, followed by others, have passed legislation outlawing this behavior. Although the laws refer to a specific abusive conduct, the shadow of brainwashing hangs over the statutes, making them difficult to enforce. Sometimes, critics argue, it is the perpetrators who accuse the victims of manipulation through coercive control (Solis 2021).

Furthermore, brainwashing was proposed after 9/11 as a folk explanation of how terrorists, some from wealthy families, had joined al-Qa'ida and later the Islamic State. Anticultists offered themselves as experts on Islamic radicalism, claiming that al-Qa'ida and other radical Muslim organizations were basically cults, which they said was also true of other non-Muslim terrorist groups. However, their lack of information on the Islamic context and on the specialized academic field of terrorism studies quickly became apparent, and they have largely been ignored by the academic community and government agencies dealing with counterterrorism (Dawson 2009).

Brainwashing theories were, however, more successful, as noted in the Introduction to this Element, as explanations of the Trump phenomenon and of how it was possible that millions of American citizens (and not a few non-Americans) supported QAnon and other movements and networks promoting wild conspiracy theories. Old hands in the anticult movement, such as former deprogrammer Steve Hassan, simply applied Singer's brainwashing theory to Trumpism and QAnon. The title of Hassan's book, *The Cult of Trump: A Leading Cult Expert Explains How the President Uses Mind Control* (Hassan 2019), already says it all. Those psychologists and psychiatrists who had maintained a concern that governments and intelligence agencies are both willing and able to heavily manipulate their citizens also revamped the idea of brainwashing, as epitomized by *Dark Persuasion: A History of Brainwashing from Pavlov to Social Media*, a book published in 2021 by Joel E. Dimsdale, a professor emeritus at University of California, San Diego (Dimsdale 2021). Dimsdale's concerns about how social media may now be used to disseminate dark propaganda and political manipulation are shared by many. However, when dealing with new religious movements, Dimsdale largely relied on the old anticult vulgate.

The bizarre claims of QAnon and the assault on Capitol Hill of January 6, 2021 lent credibility to the theory that the extreme pro-Trump fringe included victims of brainwashing, and even Hassan was taken seriously by mainline media (see, e.g., Milbank 2021). As had happened with Communist thought reform in the 1960s, and later with accusations of brainwashing directed at new religious movements, Lifton offered a more elegant version of claims that Trumpism was a cult of sorts (Lifton 2019). The fact that he had used this terminology gave credibility to the idea that the extreme right was brainwashing its followers.

Paradoxically, QAnon and similar movements were themselves persuaded that brainwashing was being used on the American political scene – by the Democratic Party, the "deep state," and what one author, who wrote an opus in no less than forty-three small volumes on the issue, called the "Marxist-Zionist-Jesuit-Masonic-Black Nobility-Illuminati-Luciferian death cult" (Hagopian 2020–21).

There was, however, a difference between how the anti-Trump and the pro-Trump camps referred to brainwashing. Critics of Trump and those who denounced QAnon as a cult basically revived the anticult model of brain-washing, based on mind control achieved through psychological manipula-tion. In QAnon, on the other hand, one would more often find, together with references to the MK-ULTRA project – which had allegedly been secretly continued by rogue deep state operatives after its official demise in 1963 – the idea that brainwashing was achieved through magic. Sometimes, it was the modern magic of mysterious mind-controlling rays directed on unsuspecting American homes from satellites, chips implanted by unscrupulous medical doctors, or drugs hidden in anti-COVID-19 vaccines by conspirators led by Bill Gates or George Soros. In other cases, QAnon postings claimed that deep state brainwashing worked by mobilizing black magic in a very traditional sense, through spells, rituals of witchcraft, human sacrifice of children, or invocations to Satan and his minions. Trump's camp always included believ-ers in magic (Asprem 2020) and denouncing Hillary Clinton and other Democratic leaders as involved in Satanism was a key part of the QAnon narrative.

In a sense, the brainwashing discourse has come full circle. The idea that those who embrace deviant beliefs had been bewitched by black magic had been secularized twice, first as hypnosis and then as brainwashing. Now, black magic with its traditional paraphernalia of sinister enchantments and Devil worship came back to be adopted by some QAnon followers as the only possible explanation why otherwise sane, patriotic, and even some Republican Americans had been persuaded, first, that Trump was up to no good, and then that he had really lost the 2020 election, rather than being cheated out of his victory by the deep state's ability to simultaneously brainwash millions of citizens.

Indeed, black magic had not disappeared when its secular version, brain-washing, became prominent. Some of the groups labeled as cults preached more or less unorthodox versions of Christianity, Hinduism, or Buddhism, but others offered esoteric and occult experiences. It was easier to accuse esoteric cults of brainwashing their victims through black magic, and once again popular culture helped persuade those who remained doubtful. In 1908, the English novelist William Somerset Maugham (1874–1965) pub-lished *The Magician*, the story of an occult master called Oliver Haddo who uses black magic to mentally enslave and then kill a naïve British girl. Maugham based Haddo on Aleister Crowley (1875–1947), known to his followers as the founder of the new religion of Thelema and to his critics as the most sinister of the esoteric cult leaders. Maugham had personally met Crowley in Paris. As evil as Haddo was in the novel, his black magic worked, Maughan claimed, and produced real brainwashing effects (Maugham 1908).

As Italian scholar Franco Pezzini (2020) has demonstrated, *The Magician* inspired dozens of lesser novels for decades, not to mention movies and comics. Crowley himself, after answering Maugham with a critical review in *Vanity Fair* that he signed "Oliver Haddo" (Haddo 1908), very much enjoyed the publicity, and even adopted some of Haddo's features as described in the novel. Haddo was also based on Svengali and, through the respected Maugham, themes introduced in the previous decade by du Maurier, who had become unmentionable in polite company because of his antisemitism, con-tinued to circulate into the twenty-first century.

Brainwashing did not totally replace black magic and hypnotism as an explanation for why weird ideas and unusual movements are held and joined by normal people. Rather, black magic, hypnotism, and brainwash-ing have continued to coexist in various combinations. I have highlighted the role of novels such as *The Magician* and *The Manchurian Candidate* because they, and their film adaptations, reached a much larger audience than scholarly studies or works of political and religious controversy. As Richardson and his colleagues noted, long-running folk beliefs transmitted through popular culture may influence politicians and courts of law. In the case of brainwashing, "the popular acceptance of the concept, coupled with its obvious utility as an 'account' of otherwise controversial behaviors, resulted in such evidence being introduced and accepted in specialty courts, including family and juvenile courts" (Reichert, Richardson, and Thomas 2015: 19).

More than seventy years after Hunter coined the word "brainwashing", we are still encountering the contradiction between the majority of academic scholars, who have largely rejected it as pseudoscience, and a popular culture where the brainwashing explanation of deviant behavior and belief remains so powerful that it refuses to go away. It comes back every time new and seemingly unexplainable forms of deviance create a market for easy explanations.

References

Abgrall, J.-M. (1996). *La Mécanique des sectes*, Paris: Payot.

Almqvist, K., Wallrup E., eds. (2005). *The Future of Religion: Perspectives from the Engelsberg Seminar 2001*, Stockholm: Axel and Margaret Ax:son Johnson Foundation.

American Psychiatric Association (1980). *Diagnostic and Statistical Manual of Mental Disorders*, 3rd ed. [DSM-III], Washington, DC: American Psychiatric Association.

American Psychiatric Association (1994). *Diagnostic and Statistical Manual of Mental Disorders*, 4th ed. [DSM-IV], Washington, DC: American Psychiatric Association.

American Psychological Association (1987a). Amicus Curiae Brief in the *Molko* Lawsuit, February 10. www.cesnur.org/testi/molko_brief.htm.

American Psychological Association (1987b). Motion to Withdraw as Amicus Curiae in the Supreme Court of the State of California Case No. SF 25038, *David Molko and Tracy Leal vs. Holy Spirit Association for the Unification of World Christianity et al.*, March 27. www.cesnur.org/testi/molko_motion .htm.

American Psychological Association (1989). Memorandum on APA's Activities regarding the *Molko* Case, July 12. www.cesnur.org/testi/APA_memo89.htm.

American Psychological Association (1996). *Report of the American Psychological Association Presidential Task Force on Violence and the Family*, Washington, DC: American Psychological Association.

Anthony, D. L. (1990). Religious Movements and "Brainwashing" Litigation: Evaluating Key Testimony. In T. Robbins and D. L. Anthony, eds., *In Gods We Trust: New Patterns of Religious Pluralism in America*, 2nd ed., New Brunswick, NJ: Transaction Publishers, pp. 295–341.

Anthony, D. L. (1996). Brainwashing and Totalitarian Influence. An Exploration of Admissibility Criteria for Testimony in Brainwashing Trials, PhD dissertation, Graduate Theological Union, Berkeley, CA.

Anthony, D. L. (1999). Pseudoscience and Minority Religions: An Evaluation of the Brainwashing Theories of Jean-Marie Abgrall. *Social Justice Research*, 12(4), 421–56.

Anthony, D. L. (2001). Tactical Ambiguity and Brainwashing Formulations: Science or Pseudoscience? In B. Zablocki and R. Thomas, eds., *Misunderstanding Cults: Searching for Objectivity in a Controversial Field*, Toronto: University of Toronto Press, pp. 215–317.

Ashcraft, W. M. (2018). *A Historical Introduction to the Study of New Religious Movements*, London: Routledge.

Asprem, E. (2020). The Magical Theory of Politics: Memes, Magic, and the Enchantment of Social Forces in the American Magic War. *Nova Religio*, 23 (4), 15–42.

Assemblée Nationale (1996). *Les Sectes en France. Rapport fait au nom de la Commission d'Enquête sur les sectes (document No. 2468)*, Paris: Les Documents d'Information de l'Assemblée nationale.

Bain, D. (1976). *The Control of Candy Jones*, Chicago, IL: Playboy Press.

Barker, E. (1984). *The Making of a Moonie: Choice or Brainwashing?* Oxford: Basil Blackwell.

Beadle, J. H. (1877). The Mormon Theocracy. *Scribner's Monthly*, 14(3), 391–97.

Biderman, A. D. (1963). *March to Calumny: The Story of American POW's in the Korean War*, New York: Macmillan.

Bowart, W. (1978). *Operation Mind Control: The CIA's Plot against America*, London: Fontana.

Brain-Washing: A Synthesis of the Russian Textbook of Psychopolitics (1955), Los Angeles, CA: Hubbard Association of Scientologists International.

Bromley, D. G. (1998). Listing (in Black and White) Some Observations on (Sociological) Thought Reform. *Nova Religio*, 1(2), 250–66.

BSERP (Board of Social and Ethical Responsibility for Psychology of the American Psychological Association) (1987). Memorandum to the Members of the Task Force on Deceptive and Indirect Methods of Persuasion and Control, May 11. www.cesnur.org/testi/APA.htm.

Cai, Congxin (2021). Church of Almighty God Members "Deprogrammed" in Jail. *Bitter Winter*, January 6. https://bitterwinter.org/church-of-almighty-god-members-deprogrammed-in-jail/.

Campion, A., Campion, J. (1999). *Holy Smoke: A Novel*, London: Bloomsbury.

Chambre des Représentants de Belgique (1997). *Enquête parlementaire visant à élaborer une politique en vue de lutter contre les pratiques illégales des sectes et les dangers qu'elles représentent pour la société et pour les personnes, particulièrement les mineurs d'âge. Rapport fait au nom de la Commission d'Enquête*, 2 vols., Brussels: Chambre des Représentants de Belgique.

Collins, A. (1997). *In the Sleep Room: The Story of the CIA Brainwashing Experiments in Canada*, 2nd ed., Toronto: Key Porter Books.

Commission pénale sur les dérives sectaires (1999). *Rapport de la Commission pénale sur les dérives sectaires sur la question de la manipulation mentale*, Geneva: Commission pénale sur les dérives sectaires.

Committee on Un-American Activities (1958). *Communist Psychological Warfare (Brainwashing): Consultation with Edward Hunter, Author and Foreign Correspondent – Committee on Un-American Activities – House of Representatives – Eighty-Fifth Congress, Second Session, March 13, 1958*, Washington, DC: United States Government Printing Office.

Condon, R. (1959). *The Manchurian Candidate*, New York: McGraw-Hill.

Corte Costituzionale (1981). Grasso. *Giurisprudenza Costituzionale*, 26, 806–34.

Corydon, B., Hubbard, L. R., Jr. (1987). *L. Ron Hubbard: Messiah or Madman?* Secaucus, NJ: Lyle Stuart.

Counts, G. S., Lodge, N. P. (1949). *Country of the Blind: The Soviet System of Mind Control*, Boston, MA: Houghton Mifflin.

Court of Appeals of California (First Appellate District, Division One) (1977). Opinion (Sims, Acting P.J.), Civ. No. 41045, *Jacqueline Katz et al. v. the Superior Court of the City and County of San Francisco*, October 6. 73 *Cal. App.* 3d 952, 969–70.

Daube, D. (1969). *Roman Law: Linguistic, Social and Philosophical Aspects*, Edinburgh: The University Press.

Dawson, L. (2009). The Study of New Religious Movements and the Radicalization of Home-Grown Terrorists: Opening a Dialogue. *Terrorism and Political Violence*, 21, 1–21.

de Certeau, M. (1990). *La Possession de Loudun*, Paris: Gallimard and Julliard.

de Lange, A. (2000). *Die Waldenser. Geschichte einer europäischen Glaubensbewegung in Bildern*, Karlsruhe: Verlag Staatsanzeiger für Baden-Württemberg.

Deutscher Bundestag (1988). *Endbericht der Enquete-Kommission "Sogenannte Sekten und Psychogruppen"*, Bonn: Deutscher Bundestag.

Di Marzio, R. (2020). "People Trapped inside Shincheonji": Broadcasting the Darker Side of Deprogramming. *Journal of CESNUR*, 4(3), 57–69.

DIMPAC (American Psychological Association Task Force on Deceptive and Indirect Techniques of Persuasion and Control) (1986). Report of the APA Task Force on Deceptive and Indirect Techniques of Persuasion and Control. www.cesnur.org/testi/DIMPAC.htm.

Dimsdale, J. E. (2021). *Dark Persuasion: A History of Brainwashing from Pavlov to Social Media*. New Haven, CT: Yale University Press.

Dulles, A. W. (1953). Brain Warfare – Russia's Secret Weapon. *US News and World Report*, May 8.

Du Maurier, G. (1894). *Trilby*, London: Osgood, McIlvaine, & Co.

Duval, P. (2012). FECRIS and Its Affiliates in France: The French Fight Against the "Capture of Souls." *Religion – Staat – Gesellschaft*, 13(2), 197–266.

Edelman, B., Richardson, J. T. (2005). Imposed Limitation on Freedom of Religion in China and the Margin of Appreciation Doctrine: A Legal Analysis of the Crackdown on the Falun Gong and Other "Evil Cults". *Journal of Church and State*, 47(2), 243–67.

Erikson, E. H. (1954). Wholeness and Totality: A Psychiatric Contribution. In C. J. Friedrich, ed., *Totalitarianism: Proceedings of a Conference Held at the American Academy of Arts and Sciences, March 1953*, Cambridge, MA: Harvard University Press, pp. 156–71.

Erikson, E. H. (1956). The Problem of Ego Identity. *Journal of the American Psychoanalytic Association*, 4, 56–121.

Estabrooks, G. H. (1943). *Hypnotism*, New York: E. P. Dutton & Company.

Fautré, W. (2012). *Japan: Abduction and Deprivation of Freedom for the Purpose of Religious De-conversion*, Brussels: Human Rights Without Frontiers.

Fautré, W. (2015). Toru Goto's Case: The Legal Saga. Human Rights Without Frontiers, October 7. http://hrwf.eu/wp-content/uploads/2015/10/Japan2015.pdf.

Fautré, W. (2020). Coercive Change of Religion in South Korea: The Case of the Shincheonji Church. *Journal of CESNUR*, 4(3), 35–56.

Fautré, W. (2021). Japan: Supreme Court to Review Case about Donations to the Unification Church. *Bitter Winter*, January 26. https://bitterwinter.org/japan-supreme-court-to-review-case-about-donations-to-the-unification-church/.

Federn, P. (1919). *Zur Psychologie der Revolution: Die vaterlose Gesellschaft*, Leipzig: Suschitzky.

Feldkeller, P. (1947). *Psycho-Politik: Zur Demokratisierung, politischen Erziehung und Säuberung*, Berlin: Chronos-Verlag.

Ferrone, V. (1989). *I profeti dell'Illuminismo. Le metamorfosi della ragione nel tardo Settecento italiano*, Rome: Laterza.

Feuerbach, L. (1841). *Das Wesen des Christentums*, Leipzig: Otto Wigand.

Freud, S. (1907). Zur sexuellen Aufklärung der Kinder (Offener Brief an Dr M. Fürst). *Soziale Medizin und Hygiene*, 2, 360–67.

Freud, S. (1927). *Die Zukunft einer Illusion*, Leipzig: Internationaler Psychoanalytischer Verlag.

Fromm E. (1941). *Escape from Freedom*, New York: Farrar & Rinehart.

Galanter, M. (1990). *Cults: Faith, Healing, and Coercion*, New York: Oxford University Press.

Gardner, R. A. (1992). *The Parental Alienation Syndrome: A Guide for Mental Health and Legal Professionals*, Cresskill, NJ: Creative Therapeutics.

Gardner, R. (2001). Book Reviews: *Destroying the World to Save It: Aum Shinrikyo, Apocalyptic Violence, and the New Global Terrorism* by Robert

Jay Lifton, and *Religious Violence in Contemporary Japan: The Case of Aum Shinrikyō*, by Ian Reader. *Monumenta Nipponica*, 56(1), 125–28.

Gardner, R. A. (2004). Commentary on Kelly and Johnston's "The Alienated Child: A Reformulation of Parental Alienation Syndrome". *Family Court Review*, 42(4), 611–21.

Gillmor, D. (1987). *I Swear by Apollo: Dr. Ewen Cameron and the CIA Brainwashing Experiments*, Montreal: Eden Press.

Ginsburg, G., Richardson, J.T. (1998). "Brainwashing" Evidence in Light of *Daubert*: Science and Unpopular Religions. In H. Reece, ed., *Law and Science: Current Legal Issues 1998, Volume I*, New York: Oxford University Press, pp. 265–88.

Givens, T. L. (1997). *The Viper on the Hearth: Mormons, Myths, and the Construction of Heresy*, New York: Oxford University Press.

Goff, K. (1948). *This Is My Story: Confessions of Stalin's Agent*, Englewood, CO: Literary Licensing.

Goff, K. (1954). *Strange Fire*, Englewood, CO: Kenneth Goff.

Goff, K. (n.d.). *Brainwashing: A Synthesis of the Russian Textbook on Psychopolitics*, Englewood, CO: Kenneth Goff.

Gordon, T. (1723). Inquiry concerning Madness, Especially Religious Madness, Called Enthusiasm. *London Journal*, April 6.

Grady, C. (1987). Opinion. Copy in the archives of CESNUR (Center for Studies on New Religions), Torino, Italy.

Groupe d'experts genevois (1997). *Audit sur les dérives sectaires. Rapport du groupe d'experts genevois au Département de la Justice et Police et des Transports du Canton de Genève*, Geneva: Éditions Suzanne Hurter.

Haack, F.-W. (1979). *Jugendreligionen: Ursachen, Trends, Reaktionen*, Munich: Claudius-Verlag.

Haddo, O. [pseudonym of Crowley, A.] (1908). How to Write a Novel! (After W. S. Maugham). *Vanity Fair* [UK edition], 30 December.

Hagopian, J. (2020–21). *Pedophilia & Empire: Satan, Sodomy & The Deep State*, 43 vols., Seattle: KDP.

Hassan, S. (2019). *The Cult of Trump: A Leading Cult Expert Explains How the President Uses Mind Control*, New York: Free Press.

Hassan, S. (2020). The BITE Model of Authoritarian Control: Undue Influence, Thought Reform, Brainwashing, Mind Control, Trafficking and the Law, PhD dissertation, Fielding Graduate University, Santa Barbara, CA.

Hill, M., Campanale, D., and Gunter, J. (2021). "Their Goal Is to Destroy Everyone": Uighur Camp Detainees Allege Systematic Rape. *BBC News*, February 3. www.bbc.com/news/world-asia-china-55794071.

Hobbes, T. (1651). *Leviathan: Or the Matter, Forme and Power of a Commonwealth, Ecclesiasticall and Civil*, London: Andrew Crooke.

Hubbard, L. R. (1951). *Science of Survival: Simplified, Faster Dianetic Techniques*, Wichita, KS: Hubbard Dianetic Foundation.

Hubbard, L. R. (1976). *The Technical Bulletins of Dianetics and Scientology, Vol. II: 1954–1956*, Copenhagen: Scientology Publications.

Hubbard, L. R. (2005). *Games Congress (Lecture Series)*. Audiotapes of the 1956 lectures, Los Angeles: Bridge Publications.

Human Rights Without Frontiers Correspondent in Russia (2012). FECRIS and Its Affiliate in Russia: The Orthodox Clerical Wing of FECRIS. *Religion – Staat – Gesellschaft*, 13(2), 267–306.

Hunter, E. (1951). *Brain-Washing in Red China: The Calculated Destruction of Men's Minds*, New York: Vanguard Press.

Hunter, E. (1956). *Brainwashing: The Story of Men Who Defied It*, New York: Farrar, Straus, and Cudahy.

Hunter E. (1957). *The Story of Mary Liu*, New York: Farrar, Straus, and Cudahy.

Hunter, E. (1958). *The Black Book on Red China: The Continuing Revolt*, New York: Bookmailer.

Hunter, E. (1960). *Brainwashing, from Pavlov to Powers*, New York: Bookmailer.

Hunter, E. (1975). Timely Book. *Tactics*, 12(12), December 20, 7–10.

Introvigne, M. (1993). Strange Bedfellows or Future Enemies? *Update & Dialog*, 3, 13–22.

Introvigne, M. (1999). Deprogramming Kate Winslet: A Review of "Holy Smoke," by Anna and Jane Campion. www.cesnur.org/testi/holysmoke.htm.

Introvigne, M. (2014a). Scientology in Italy: Plagio and the Twenty Year Legal Saga. In J. T. Richardson and F. Bellanger, eds., *Legal Cases, New Religious Movements, and Minority Faiths*, Farnham, UK: Ashgate, pp. 25–36.

Introvigne, M. (2014b). Advocacy, Brainwashing Theories, and New Religious Movements. *Religion*, 44(2), 303–319.

Introvigne, M. (2017). Did L. Ron Hubbard Believe in Brainwashing? The Strange Story of the "Brain-Washing Manual" of 1955. *Nova Religio: The Journal of Alternative and Emergent Religions*, 20(4), 62–79.

Introvigne, M. (2018). *Xie Jiao* as "Criminal Religious Movements": A New Look at Cult Controversies in China and around the World. *Journal of CESNUR*, 2(1), 13–32.

Introvigne, M. (2020). Deception, New Religious Movements, and Claims for Damages: The Case of *H.E. et al. v Seosan Church of Shincheonji et al. Journal of CESNUR*, 4(4), 49–68.

Introvigne, M., Mayer J.-F. (2002). Occult Masters and the Temple of Doom: The Fiery End of the Solar Temple. In D. G. Bromley and J. G. Melton, eds.,

Cults, Religion and Violence, Cambridge: Cambridge University Press, pp. 170–88.

Jay, M. (1973). *The Dialectical Imagination: A History of the Frankfurt School and the Institute of Social Research 1923–1950*, Boston, MA: Little, Brown and Company.

Johnston, J. R., Kelly, J. B. (2004). Rejoinder to Gardner's "Commentary on Kelly and Johnston's 'The Alienated Child: A Reformulation of Parental Alienation Syndrome'". *Family Court Review*, 42(4), 622–28.

Kant, I. (1793). *Die Religion innerhalb der Grenzen der bloßen Vernunft*. Königsberg: Friedrich Nicolovius.

Kelly, J. B., Johnston, J. R. (2001). The Alienated Child: A Reformulation of Parental Alienation Syndrome. *Family Court Review*, 39(3), 249–66.

Kent, S. A. (2000), *Gehirnwäsche im Rehabilitation Project Force (RPF) der Scientology-Organisation*, Hamburg: Freie und Hansestadt Hamburg – Behörde für Inneres – Arbeitsgruppe Scientology und Landeszentrale für politische Bildung.

KKNews (2017). "反邪動態」美國、義大利專家赴鄭州進行反邪教學術交流" ["Anti-Cult": US, Italian Experts Went to Zhengzhou for Anti-Cult Academic Exchanges], July 11. https://kknews.cc/society/rrr2m8o.html.

Kominsky, M. (1970). *The Hoaxers: Plain Liars, Fancy Liars, and Damned Liars*, Boston, MA: Branden Press.

Lee, B. X., ed. (2017). *The Dangerous Case of Donald Trump: 27 Psychiatrists and Mental Health Experts Assess a President*, New York: Thomas Dunne Books.

Lifton, R. J. (1961). *Thought Reform and the Psychology of Totalism: A Study of "Brainwashing" in China*, New York: Norton.

Lifton, R. J. (1987a). *The Future of Immortality and Other Essays for a Nuclear Age*, New York: Basic Books.

Lifton, R. J. (1987b). *The Nazi Doctors: Medical Killing and the Psychology of Genocide*, New York: Basic Books.

Lifton, R. J. (1995). Foreword. In Singer, M. T., Lalich, J., *Cults in Our Midst*. San Francisco, CA: Jossey-Bass, pp. XI–XIII.

Lifton, R. J. (1999). *Destroying the World to Save It: Aum Shinrikyo, Apocalyptic Violence, and the New Global Terrorism*, New York: Henry Holt and Company.

Lifton, R. J. (2019). *Losing Reality: On Cults, Cultism, and the Mindset of Political and Religious Zealotry*, New York: The New Press.

Lifton, R. J., Falk, R. (1982). *Indefensible Weapons: The Political and Psychological Case against Nuclearism*, New York: Basic Books.

Lockridge, R., Estabrooks, G. H. (1945). *Death in the Mind*, New York: E. P. Dutton & Company.

Malony, H. N. (1996). *Brainwashing and Religion: The 1996 Integration Lectures of The Graduate School of Psychology, Fuller Theological Seminary*, Pasadena, CA: Fuller Theological Seminary.

Marks, J. (1979). *The Search for the "Manchurian Candidate,"* New York: Times Books.

Marx, K. (1844). Zur Kritik der Hegelschen Rechts-Philosophie. *Deutsch-französische Jahrbücher*, 1–2, 71–85.

Maugham, W. S. (1908). *The Magician*. London: Heinemann.

Meerloo, A. M. (1944). *Total War and the Human Mind: A Psychologist's Experience in Occupied Holland*, London: The Netherlands Government Information Bureau and George Allen & Unwin.

Meerloo, A. M. (1949). *Delusion and Mass-Delusion*, New York: Nervous and Mental Disease Monographs.

Meerloo, A. M. (1951). The Crime of Menticide. *American Journal of Psychiatry*, 107, 594–98.

Meerloo, A. M. (1956). *The Rape of the Mind: The Psychology of Thought Control and Brainwashing*, Cleveland, OH: World Publishing Company.

Meerloo, A. M. (1957). *Mental Seduction and Menticide: The Psychology of Thought Control and Brainwashing*, London: Jonathan Cape.

Meerloo, A. M. (1960). *The Dance: From Ritual to Rock 'n Roll – Ballet to Ballroom*, New York: Chilton.

Meerloo, A. M. (1962). *Suicide and Mass Suicide*, New York: E. P. Dutton & Company.

Meerloo. A. M. (1971). *Intuition and the Evil Eye: The Natural History of a Superstition*, Wassenaar, Netherlands: Servire.

Melton, J. G. 2018. A Contemporary Ordered Religious Community: The Sea Organization. *Journal of CESNUR*, 2(2), 21–59.

Milbank, D. (2021). Trump Is Gone, but Marjorie Taylor Greene Is Keeping Up the Cult. *Washington Post*, January 22.

Moravia, A., Eco, U., Gatti, A., et al. (1969). *Sotto il nome di plagio*. Milan: Bompiani.

Motilla, A. (1999). *New Religious Movements and the Law in the European Union: Proceedings of the Meeting, Universidade Moderna, Lisbon, 8–9 November 1997*, Milan: Giuffrè.

Murariu, M. (2017). *Totality, Charisma, Authority*, Wiesbaden: Springer.

Ofshe, R., Singer, M. (1986). Attacks on Central vs. Peripheral Elements of Self and the Impact of Thought Reforming Techniques. *Cultic Studies Journal*, 3 (1), 3–24.

Ogliaro, D. (2003). *Gratia et Certamen: The Relationship between Grace and Free Will in the Discussion of Augustine with the So-Called Semipelagians*, Leuven: Leuven University Press.

Orwell, G. (1949). *1984*, London: Secker & Warburg.

Palmer, D. A. (2012). Heretical Doctrines, Reactionary Secret Societies, Evil Cults: Labelling Heterodoxy in 20th-Century China. In M. Yang, ed., *Chinese Religiosities: The Vicissitudes of Modernity and State Formation*, Berkeley, CA: University of California Press, pp. 113–34.

Palmer, S. J. (2011). *The New Heretics of France: Minority Religions, la République, and the Government-sponsored "War on Sects,"* New York: Oxford University Press.

Pasley, V. S. (1955). *Twenty-One Stayed: The Stories of the American GIs Who Chose Communist China, Who They Were and Why They Stayed*, New York: Farrar, Straus & Cudahy.

Patrick, T. (1976). *Let Our Children Go!* Boston, MA: E. P. Dutton & Company.

Pezzini, F. (2020). *Le nozze chimiche di Aleister Crowley. Itinerari letterari con la Grande Bestia*, Città di Castello: Odoya.

Pick, D. (2000). *Svengali's Web: The Alien Enchanter in Modern Culture*, New Haven, CT: Yale University Press.

Reich, W. (1933). *Die Massenpsychologie des Faschismus*, Copenhagen: Verlag für Sexualpolitik.

Reichert, J., Richardson, J. T., and Thomas, R. (2015). "Brainwashing": Diffusion of a Questionable Concept in Legal Systems. *International Journal for the Study of New Religions*, 6(1), 3–26.

Richardson, J. T. (1978). An Oppositional and General Conceptualization of Cult. *Annual Review of the Social Sciences of Religion*, 2, 29–52.

Richardson, J. T. (1993a). Definitions of Cult: From Sociological-Technical to Popular-Negative. *Review of Religious Research*, 34(4), 348–56.

Richardson, J. T. (1993b). Religiosity as Deviance: Negative Religious Bias in and Misuse of the DSM-III. *Deviant Behavior: An Interdisciplinary Journal*, 14(1), 1–21.

Richardson, J. T. (1993c). A Social Psychological Critique of "Brainwashing" Claims about Recruitment to New Religions. In D. G. Bromley and J. K. Hadden, eds., *The Handbook of Cults and Sects in America*, Greenwich, CT: JAI Press, pp. 75–97.

Richardson, J. T. (1996a). Sociology and the New Religions: "Brainwashing," the Courts, and Religious Freedom. In P. J. Jenkins and S. Kroll-Smith, eds., *Witnessing for Sociology: Sociologists in Court*, Westport, CT: Praeger, pp. 115–37.

Richardson, J. T. (1996b). "Brainwashing" Claims and Minority Religions outside the United States: Cultural Diffusion of a Questionable Concept in the Legal Arena. *Brigham Young University Law Review*, 4, 873–904.

Richardson, J. T. (2011). Deprogramming: From Private Self-Help to Governmental Organized Repression. *Crime, Law and Social Change*, 55, 321–36.

Richardson, J. T. (2014). "Brainwashing" as Forensic Evidence. In S. J. Morewitz and M. L. Goldstein, eds., *Handbook of Forensic Sociology and Psychology*, New York: Springer, pp. 77–85.

Richardson, J. T. (2015). "Brainwashing" and Mental Health. In H. S. Friedman, ed., *Encyclopedia of Mental Health*, 2nd ed., New York: Elsevier, pp. 210–15.

Richardson, J. T., Introvigne, M. (2001). "Brainwashing" Theories in European Parliamentary and Administrative Reports on "Cults" and "Sects". *Journal for Scientific Study of Religion*, 40(2), 143–68.

Richardson, J. T., Ginsburg G. P., Gatowski S. I., and Dobbin, S. A. (1995). The Problems of Applying *Daubert* to Psychological Syndrome Evidence. *Judicature*, 79, 10–16.

SAC Los Angeles (1956). Office Memorandum to Director, FBI. April 17. http://scientology-research.org/wp/wp-content/uploads/2017/11/17-cv -03842-A-210-279.pdf.

Sargant, W. (1957). *Battle for the Mind: A Physiology of Conversion and Brainwashing*, New York: Doubleday.

Sargant, W. (1967). *The Unquiet Mind: The Autobiography of a Physician in Psychological Medicine*, Boston, MA: Little, Brown and Company.

Sargant, W. (1971) *Battle for the Mind: A Physiology of Conversion and Brainwashing*, 3rd ed., New York: Perennial Library.

Scheflin, A. W., Opton, E. M., Jr. (1978). *The Mind Manipulators: A Non-Fiction Account*, New York: Paddington.

Schein, E. H. (1956). The Chinese Indoctrination Program for Prisoners of War. *Psychiatry*, 19, 149–72.

Schein, E. H. (1985). *Organizational Culture and Leadership*, San Francisco, CA: Jossey-Bass.

Schein, E.H. (1993). The Academic as Artist: Personal and Professional Roots. In A. G. Bedeian, ed., *Management Laureates: A Collection of Autobiographical Essays (Volume 3)*, Greenwood, CT: JAI Press, pp. 31–62.

Schein, E. H., Schneier, I., and Barker, C. H. (1961). *Coercive Persuasion: A Socio-Psychological Analysis of the "Brainwashing" of American Civilian Prisoners by the Chinese Communists*, New York: W. W. Norton & Company.

Schein, E. H., Singer, M. T. (1992). Follow-Up Intelligence Data on Prisoners Repatriated from North Korea. *Psychological Reports*, 11, 93–194.

Seed, D. (2004). *Brainwashing: The Fictions of Mind Control. A Study of Novels and Films since World War II*, Kent, OH: Kent State University Press.

Shaftesbury, A. A. C. (1708). *A Letter concerning Enthusiasm*, London: J. Morphew.

Shterin, M.S., Richardson, J.T. (2000). Effects of the Western Anti-Cult Movement on Development of Laws concerning Religion in Post-Communist Russia. *Journal of Church and State* 42(2), 247–271.

Shupe, A. D. (1995). *In the Name of All That's Holy: A Theory of Clergy Malfeasance*, Westport, CT: Praeger.

Shupe, A. D. (2007). *Spoils of the Kingdom: Clergy Misconduct and Religious Community*, Urbana, IL: University of Illinois Press.

Shupe, A. D., Bromley, D. G. (1980). *The New Vigilantes: Deprogrammers, Anti-Cultists, and the New Religions*, Beverly Hills, CA: SAGE.

Shupe, A. D., Bromley, D. G., eds. (1994). *Anti-Cult Movements in Cross-Cultural Perspective*, New York: Garland.

Shupe, A. D., Darnell, S. E. (2006). *Agents of Discord: Deprogramming, Pseudo-Science, and the American Anticult Movement*, New Brunswick, NJ: Transaction Publishers.

Singer, M. T., Lalich, J. (1995). *Cults in Our Midst*, San Francisco, CA: Jossey-Bass.

Singer, M. T., Ofshe, R. (1990). Thought Reform Programs and the Production of Psychiatric Casualties. *Psychiatric Annals*, 20(4), 188–93.

Singer, M. T., Ofshe, R. (1994). Summons and Complaint against the American Psychological Association et al., filed with the Superior Court of the State of California in and for the County of Alameda on January 31, 1994. Copy in the archives of CESNUR (Center for Studies on New Religions), Torino, Italy.

Singer, M. T., Schein, E. H. (1958). Projective Test Responses of Prisoners of Wars following Repatriation. *Psychiatry*, 21, 375–85.

Solis, M. (2021). Do "Coercive Control" Laws Really Help Abuse Victims? *The Cut*, February 2. www.thecut.com/2021/02/coercive-control-laws-domestic-abuse.html.

Stark, R. (1996). *The Rise of Christianity: A Sociologist Reconsiders History*, Princeton, NJ: Princeton University Press.

Stein, A. (2002). *Inside Out: A Memoir of Entering and Breaking Out of a Minneapolis Political Cult*, Saint Cloud, MN: North Star Press.

Stein, A. (2016). *Terror, Love and Brainwashing: Attachment in Cults and Totalitarian Systems*, London: Routledge.

Strassman, H., Thaler, M., and Schein, E. H. (1956). A Prisoner of War Syndrome: Apathy as a Reaction to Severe Stress. *American Journal of Psychiatry*, 12, 998–1002.

Superior Court of the State of California in and for the County of Alameda (1994). Order (Lambden J.), Case No. 730012–8, *Margaret Singer et al. v. American Psychological Association et al.*, June 17. www.cesnur.org/testi/ singer.htm.

Supreme Court of the State of California (1988). Opinion (Mosk J.), Case No. SF 25038, *David Molko and Tracy Leal v. Holy Spirit Association for the Unification of World Christianity et al.* October 17, 46 *Cal.3d* 1092, 762.

Taves, A. (1999). *Fits, Trances and Visions: Experiencing Religion and Explaining Experience from Wesley to James*, Princeton, NJ: Princeton University Press.

Thomas, D. (1986). Letter from Dorothy Thomas, Executive Assistant, BSERP, December 29. Copy in the archives of CESNUR (Center for Studies on New Religions), Torino, Italy.

Thomas, G. (1989). *Journey into Madness: The True Story of Secret CIA Mind Control and Medical Abuse*, New York: Bantam Books.

Thomas, R. T., Richardson, J. T. (2015). Parental Alienation Syndrome: 30 Years On and Still Junk Science. *Judge's Journal*, 54(3), 22, 24.

United States Court of Appeals, District of Columbia Circuit (1988). Opinion (Buckley J.), Case Nos. 87–7033, 87–7060, *Robert Kropinsky v. World Plan Execution Council – US et al.*, August 5, 853 *F.2d* 948.

United States Court of Appeals for the Ninth Circuit (1998). Opinion (Beezer J), Case No. 96–35050, *Jason Scott v. Rick Ross et al. and Cult Awareness Network*, April 8. https://caselaw.findlaw.com/us-9th-circuit/1097138 .html.

United States District Court for the Northern District of California (1990). Opinion (Jensen J.), Case No. CR-88–0616 DLJ, *United States v. Steven Fishman*, April 13, 743 *F. Supp.* 713.

United States District Court for the Southern District of New York (1993). Order, Case No. 92CV6082, *Margaret Singer and Richard Ofshe v. American Psychological Association et al.*, August 9, *W.L.* 307782 S.D.N.Y.

Usai, A. (1996). *Profili penali dei condizionamenti psichici. Riflessioni sui problemi penali posti dalla fenomenologia dei nuovi movimenti religiosi*, Milan: Giuffrè.

USCIRF (United States Commission on International Religious Freedom) (2020). The Anti-Cult Movement and Religious Regulation in Russia and the Former Soviet Union. www.uscirf.gov/sites/default/files/2020%20Anti-Cult%20Update%20-%20Religious%20Regulation%20in%20Russia.pdf.

Ward, M. (1855). *Female Life among the Mormons*, London: Routledge.

Weinstein, H. M. (1990). *Psychiatry and the CIA: Victims of Mind Control*, Washington, DC: American Psychiatric Press.

West, L. J. (1989). Persuasive Techniques in Contemporary Cults: A Public Health Approach. In M. Galanter, ed., *Cults and New Religious Movements*, Washington, DC: American Psychiatric Association, pp. 165–92.

Winter, A. (1998). *Mesmerized: Powers of Mind in Victorian Britain*, Chicago: University of Chicago Press.

Witteveen, T. A. 1984. *Overheide en Nieuwe Religieuze Bewegingen*. Groningen: Rijksuniversiteit Groningen.

Wolff, H., Hinkle, L. (1956). Communist Interrogation and Indoctrination of "Enemies of the State." *Archives of Neurology and Psychiatry*, 76, 115–74.

Wu, J. (2016). Words and Concepts in Chinese Religious Denunciation: A Study of the Genealogy of *Xiejiao. Chinese Historical Review*, 23(1), 1–22.

Wu, J. (2017). *Mandarins and Heretics: The Constructions of "Heresy" in Chinese State Discourse*, Leiden: Brill.

Yandell, K. E. (1990). *Hume's "Inexplicable Mystery" – His Views on Religion*, Philadelphia, PA: Temple University Press.

Zablocki, B. (1997). The Blacklisting of a Concept: The Strange History of the Brainwashing Conjecture in the Sociology of Religion. *Nova Religio*, 1(1), 96–121.

Zablocki, B. (1998). Exit Cost Analysis: A New Approach to the Scientific Study of Brainwashing. *Nova Religio*, 1(2), 216–49.

Zhang, X. (2020). The Potential Illegitimacy of the PRC's Effort to Distinguish *Xie Jiao* from "Cult" or "Destructive Cult." *Alternative Spirituality and Religion Review*, 11(1), 81–95.

Cambridge Elements

New Religious Movements

James R. Lewis

Wuhan University

James R. Lewis is Professor of Philosophy at Wuhan University, China. He currently edits or co-edits four book series, is the general editor for the *Alternative Spirituality and Religion Review* and the associate editor for the *Journal of Religion and Violence*. His publications include *The Cambridge Companion to Religion and Terrorism* (Cambridge University Press 2017) and *Falun Gong: Spiritual Warfare and Martyrdom* (Cambridge University Press 2018).

Rebecca Moore

San Diego State University

Rebecca Moore is Emerita Professor of Religious Studies at San Diego State University. She has written numerous books and articles on Peoples Temple and the Jonestown tragedy. Publications include *Beyond Brainwashing: Perspectives on Cultic Violence* (Cambridge University Press 2018) and *Peoples Temple and Jonestown in the Twenty-First Century* (Cambridge University Press 2022). She is reviews editor for *Nova Religio*, the quarterly journal on new and emergent religions published by University of California Press.

About the Series

Elements in New Religious Movements go beyond cult stereotypes and popular prejudices to present new religions and their adherents in a scholarly and engaging manner. Case studies of individual groups, such as Transcendental Meditation and Scientology, provide in-depth consideration of some of the most well known, and controversial, groups. Thematic examinations of women, children, science, technology, and other topics focus on specific issues unique to these groups. Historical analyses locate new religions in specific religious, social, political, and cultural contexts. These examinations demonstrate why some groups exist in tension with the wider society and why others live peaceably in the mainstream. The series demonstrates the differences, as well as the similarities, within this great variety of religious expressions. To discuss contributing to this series please contact Professor Moore.

Cambridge Elements ☰

New Religious Movements

Elements in the Series

The Sound Current Tradition: A Historical Overview
David Christopher Lane

Brainwashing: Reality or Myth?
Massimo Introvigne

L. Ron Hubbard and Scientology Studies
Donald A. Westbrook

A full series listing is available at: www.cambridge.org/ENRM

Printed in the United States
by Baker & Taylor Publisher Services

Cambridge Elements ≡

Elements on Women in the History of Philosophy
edited by
Jacqueline Broad
Monash University

SIMONE DE BEAUVOIR

Karen Green
University of Melbourne

CAMBRIDGE
UNIVERSITY PRESS

University Printing House, Cambridge CB2 8BS, United Kingdom

One Liberty Plaza, 20th Floor, New York, NY 10006, USA

477 Williamstown Road, Port Melbourne, VIC 3207, Australia

314–321, 3rd Floor, Plot 3, Splendor Forum, Jasola District Centre, New Delhi – 110025, India

103 Penang Road, #05–06/07, Visioncrest Commercial, Singapore 238467

Cambridge University Press is part of the University of Cambridge.

It furthers the University's mission by disseminating knowledge in the pursuit of education, learning, and research at the highest international levels of excellence.

www.cambridge.org
Information on this title: www.cambridge.org/9781009011785
DOI: 10.1017/9781009026802

© Karen Green 2022

This publication is in copyright. Subject to statutory exception and to the provisions of relevant collective licensing agreements, no reproduction of any part may take place without the written permission of Cambridge University Press.

First published 2022

A catalogue record for this publication is available from the British Library.

ISBN 978-1-009-01178-5 Paperback
ISSN 2634-4645 (online)
ISSN 2634-4637 (print)

Cambridge University Press has no responsibility for the persistence or accuracy of URLs for external or third-party internet websites referred to in this publication and does not guarantee that any content on such websites is, or will remain, accurate or appropriate.

Simone de Beauvoir

Elements on Women in the History of Philosophy

DOI: 10.1017/9781009026802
First published online: July 2022

Karen Green
University of Melbourne

Author for correspondence: Karen Green, karen.green@unimelb.edu.au

Abstract: Tracing her intellectual development from her university years, when she was trained in a Cartesian and neo-Kantian philosophical tradition, to her final decade, during which she was recognised as having inspired the emerging strands of late twentieth-century feminism, Beauvoir is shown to have been among the most influential philosophical voices of the mid-twentieth century. Countering the recent trend to read her in isolation from Sartre, she is shown to have adopted, adapted, and influenced his philosophy, most importantly through encouraging him to engage with Hegel and to consider our relations with others. *The Second Sex* is read in the light of her existentialist humanism and ultimately faulted for having succumbed too uncritically to the masculine myth that it is men who are solely responsible for society's intellectual and cultural history.

Keywords: feminism, existentialism, Jean-Paul Sartre, phenomenology, Marxism

© Karen Green 2022

ISBNs: 9781009011785 (PB), 9781009026802 (OC)
ISSNs: 2634-4645 (online), 2634-4637 (print)

Contents

1 Beauvoir before Sartre   1

2 Sartre and the Discovery of Hegel   7

3 *The Second Sex*   23

4 Autobiography and Politics   43

5 Beauvoir's Impact   51

List of Abbreviations of Works by Beauvoir   58

References   61

1 Beauvoir before Sartre

Born in 1908, Simone de Beauvoir was an early beneficiary of women's nineteenth-century campaigns for access to higher education. From 1926 to 1929, she studied for and gained the *agrégation* (the qualification for becoming a philosophy teacher) on nearly equal terms with a group of young men of her generation – Maurice Merleau-Ponty, Claude Lévi-Strauss, Paul Nizan, René Maheu, Raymond Aron, and Jean-Paul Sartre – who, collectively, would become dominating influences on mid-twentieth-century French philosophy. She was particularly lucky in having been able to compete as an equal with this group of ambitious young men, for women had only been admitted to study for the *agrégation* in 1924, and by the late 1930s, the exam was segregated, thus for many decades confining women to success in what was taken to be an inferior female league (Imbert, 2004; Moi, 1994, 50–4).

Beauvoir's philosophy developed in conversation with these male contemporaries, whose preoccupations arose from a philosophical background that she shared. Merleau-Ponty's most influential book was *Phenomenology of Perception* (1945), which attempts to characterise our perception of the external world, avoiding both empiricism, which postulates immediate causal relationships with sensory atoms (sense-data), and an intellectualism, which assumes that we have perceptual access to rationally comprehensible forms. He was deeply influenced both by Husserl's phenomenology and by gestalt psychology. Lévi-Strauss is remembered for *The Elementary Structures of Kinship* (1949), which introduced structuralism and Marxism into anthropology, interpreting the mental structures and kinship relations of pre-colonial peoples through a series of dualistic oppositions and as economic relationships, in which the exchange of women is exemplary. Less famous as a philosopher, but a Marxist author of novels in the tradition of 'committed literature' to which Jean-Paul Sartre also contributed, Paul Nizan was an active communist, unlike the anti-communist Raymond Aron, who saw early the similarity between Fascism and Stalinism and is remembered as an important figure in French liberalism.[1] Of this group, only René Maheu failed to leave behind a substantial legacy of publications. An early advocate of individualism, he became director general of UNESCO in 1961, evincing, like his friends, a political commitment on an international level. Demonstrating similar concerns to these contemporaries, Sartre's major work, *Being and Nothingness* (1943), explores the nature of consciousness and its relationship to the external world and to human freedom, while his *Critique of Dialectical Reason* (1961) attempts to fuse the existentialism of this earlier

---

[1] By 1955, Beauvoir includes him in her criticism of right-wing thinkers (*PolW*, 117, 127, 138).

work with Marxist concepts of historical dialectic, class consciousness, and ideology.

The works of the generation to which Beauvoir belonged thus cluster around two axes. One involves questions of the nature of the mind, perception, or consciousness, its relationship to reality, and the conflict between realism and idealism – issues that they inherited from a philosophical education deeply indebted to René Descartes's sceptical challenge, solved by the *cogito*, according to which we cannot doubt that our consciousness exists. Descartes's solution to scepticism results in his adoption of a problematic metaphysical dualism that divides mind and body into two causally disjoint substances. In the wake of Descartes and Kant, the teachers of Beauvoir's generation, who included Léon Brunschvicg and Alain (Émile-August Chartier), were Cartesian rationalists who tended towards a neo-Kantian idealism, against which Sartre, in particular, revolted. By contrast, Beauvoir was initially attracted to an idealist acceptance of the reality of mind, rather than matter, and for a time found Brunschvicg's ideas compatible with her own (*DPS2*, September 27, 1928, October 24, 1928; *CJ*, 463, 501; *MD*, 207).

The other axis that preoccupied members of this generation concerned the political sphere, the lead up to and experience of the Second World War, the fight against Fascism, and the legacy of Marxism. They had largely rejected the existence of God, so important for the Cartesian solution to scepticism, yet were still working with the legacy of Descartes and Kant, while attempting to approach traditional metaphysical, epistemological, and ethical problems from resolutely anti-theological grounds. Their philosophy was distinctive in beginning from the experience of existing in a world of sensible phenomena. As a result, Beauvoir, Merleau-Ponty, and Sartre earned the reputation of being existentialists and phenomenologists. Indeed, Sartre's *Being and Nothingness* is subtitled *An Essay on Phenomenological Ontology*, thus, like Merleau-Ponty's *Phenomenology of Perception*, advertising its debt to Husserl and Heidegger's phenomenology, which they exploited and developed, without being particularly faithful to the intentions or conclusions of either of these German thinkers. The label 'existentialist', however, was one that was only applied to their works after the Second World War. It captured, in particular, the thought, which Beauvoir attributes to Heidegger and which Sartre develops in his own way in *Being and Nothingness*, that 'existence precedes essence'. That is to say, the existence of consciousness implies its essence; our nature is not something that precedes us – found, for instance, eternally in the mind of God – but is something that comes into being as a result of our existing (*PCe*, 123; Heidegger, 1962, I.i.§9, 67; Sartre, 1975, 348; 1993, Introduction, §3, xxxi).

The attitudes that make up the popular understanding of existentialism – denial of the existence of God, the consequent problem of the meaninglessness of human existence, and the absurdity of being – had been adopted by Beauvoir well before she met up with Sartre and his friends (*MD*, 228–9). Already in her first years of studying philosophy she was reading Schopenhauer, choosing to quote in her diary from his *World as Will and Representation*, 'Existence itself, is a constant suffering, and is partly woeful, partly fearful' (*CJ*, May 9, 1927, 336; *DPS*, 252; Schopenhauer, 1958, 3. §52.267). These diaries show her struggling with an all too common adolescent angst, vacillating between a somewhat arrogant confidence in her intellectual capacity and a sense of oppression by the demands of life. She laments 'the metaphysical anxiety of man alone in the unknown' (*CJ*, September 4, 1927, 403; *DPS*, 309). But she also already demonstrates a sense of responsibility for what she makes of herself:

> I must affirm to myself that the truth is in my strength and not in my weakness, that this evening I am right, and not in the morning when upon opening my eyes, the anxiety of having to live again oppresses me even when the day's program is attractive. (*CJ*, May 21, 1927, 349; *DPS*, 263)

Another influence, at this stage of her life, is the now almost entirely forgotten philosophy of Jules Lagneau, who had had a considerable influence on the philosopher Alain. She finds Lagneau's expression 'I have no support but my absolute despair' beautiful (*CJ*, May 21, 1927, 348; *DPS*, 262). Already, she is committed to an attitude to life that will re-emerge in a more sophisticated form in her later writing, saying,

> But knowing that this noumenal world exists, that I cannot attain, in which alone it can be explained to me why I live, I will build my life in the phenomenal world, which is nevertheless not negligible. I will take myself as an end. (*CJ*, May 21, 1927, 348; *DPS*, 262)

This renunciation of the possibility of justification coming from the world beyond human experience, an external absolute, or things as they are in themselves (the noumenal world) and its replacement with a self-justification grounded in experience (the phenomenal world) will re-emerge in more sophisticated form in Beauvoir's later writing. The sense of the urgency of the question 'Why do I exist?' remains a theme even in her last novella, *Les Belles Images*, in which she puts this question in the mouth of a child and questions the capacity of consumerist society to offer an adequate response (*BIe*, 20).

The philosophy of Henri Bergson is also important for Beauvoir's early philosophical formation (Simons, 2003). She takes from him the view that words, with their 'well-defined outlines', cannot capture 'the delicate and fugitive impressions of our individual consciousness', a thought that will also recur in her later fiction (*CJ*, August 13, 1926, 57; *DPS*, 58). This sense, that each private consciousness is closed in on itself and can never directly communicate with the consciousness of another, is part of the legacy of Descartes. It is a consequence of his dualism that while each of us knows immediately that we are thinking things, and so knows that our own ideas and impressions of the world exist, the minds of others cannot be immediately accessed. The problem of solipsism, the question of how we can know that we are not the one and only consciousness, thus looms large. Communicating with others, through the use of public, material signs, cannot give us full access to the other's private interiority. It may be because Beauvoir was already interested in this problem that her teacher, Brunschvicg, encouraged her to write a dissertation on Leibniz, who, in his *Monadology*, accepts that each individual perspective on the world is shut off from the other, constituting a 'windowless monad' that can only know its own ideas or subjective perceptions (*MD*, 266). To explain the correspondence that exists between our perceptions and those of other people, Leibniz proposes that God coordinates all the individual perspectives in harmony, so that we acquire the illusion of existing in an objectively existing material world. Beauvoir says little about this dissertation in her diaries but seems dissatisfied with Leibniz, which is understandable, given that she had lost her faith in God. So, the problem of solipsism continued to loom large for her, and she remained for some time a solipsist (*WD*, 320). The temptation to adopt a solipsistic attitude towards the world will be a feature of central characters in many of her novels. They will only be wrenched out of their solipsism by being forced to recognise the existence of the consciousness of others as it impinges on their own self-assessment and projects.

As well as tracing her philosophical formation, her student diaries are dominated by two themes that are not inherited from this philosophical background. The first is love, in particular her love for her cousin, Jacques Champigneulles, and the second the related question of our relations with others. In the autobiography that she began publishing in her fiftieth year, the relationship with Jacques plays a relatively minor role, while her friendship with Elizabeth Lacoin, whom she calls Elizabeth Mabille, or 'Zaza', enters earlier into the account of her youth and extends throughout the narrative (*MD*, 91–6). By contrast, Jacques is presented as a cousin whom her family thought she might marry, and whom she believed, on and off, that she loved, but who also annoyed her (*MD*, 198–211, 232–4, 241–3, 263–4). Yet it is clear from the diaries she kept from 1926 to 1929 that her infatuation with him occupied a dominant, even obsessive, place in her mental life and developing sense of self during this period. She begins by being 'completely involved in the great joy' of this friendship and feeling that they have a mutual understanding, a communion of souls (*CJ*, October 29, 1926, 148; *DPS*, 142). By

November 1926, her soul's 'mystical attraction' to his soul demands a love that will never die (*CJ*, November 16, 1926, 193; *DPS*, 180). He introduced her to Alain-Fournier's novel *Le Grand Meaulnes*, and she identifies him with its eponymous hero (*MD*, 201). Her experience and account of this relationship is mediated through the works she was then reading, in particular the correspondence between Jacques Rivière and Alain-Fournier (Rivière & Alain-Fournier, 1926–8). Echoing the tortured self-affirmation of the first and the nostalgic romanticism of the second, her prose is particularly reminiscent of Alain-Fournier when she evokes soft summer evenings and tender moments shared in the Luxembourg Gardens. Rivière, who came from Bordeaux, near where she spent holidays at the Beauvoir family estate of Meyrignac, had a special significance for her, being closely bound up with her infatuation with Jacques. Rivière had been secretary of the *Nouvelle Revue Française* between 1912 and 1914, and then editor from 1919 to 1925, and through his literary criticism he introduced Beauvoir's generation to the works of Marcel Proust, Paul Valéry, Sigmund Freud, Fyodor Dostoevsky, and Éluard Mauriac. She later notes that when young she hardly read anything other than the writers associated with this review (*MD*, 229). It was during this period of infatuation with Jacques that she was developing her literary taste and orientation, reading and quoting from these and other similar authors, such as Paul Claudel, Maurice Barrès, André Gide, and Rainer Maria Rilke. These were members of a generation of writers whom she later characterised as having 'refused to accept the wisdom of their elders' but who 'did not attempt to find another to take its place' (*MD*, 194). Her love for this literature, which is bound up with this first early love, will endure. Traces abound in her novels as well as in her later analyses of the situation of women. Yet she would attempt to go beyond these writers by offering something to replace the traditional moralism they had rejected.

Many years later, when feminist scholars were beginning to disengage Beauvoir's ideas from those of Sartre, whose reputation and philosophy had, during the initial critical reception of their works, completely engulfed and overshadowed hers, Jessica Benjamin extracted from her the admission that, indeed, 'the problem of the consciousness of the Other, was my problem' (Benjamin & Simons, 1999, 10). The student diaries confirm that from very early on Beauvoir was drawn to the theme of 'this opposition of self and other that I felt upon starting to live' (*CJ*, July 10, 1927, 367; *DPS*, 279). In the diaries, the confused ideas that she expresses on the question of self and other are often tied to her ruminations over her relationship with Jacques, who continued to prey on her mind well into 1929. At this stage, as well as sometimes feeling a solipsistic alienation from others, she also expressed a need, in order to achieve an authentic sense of self, to depend on someone who loved her:

> There is only one being who might give me back the authentic consciousness
> of myself, only one being who might define me and be the resistance for me to
> lean on, receiving my imprint, not this emptiness that lets me pass by without
> identifying traits that I seek almost with anxiety. I have hungered and thirsted
> for you, Jacques, these past few days, when I say words, there is no response,
> but sometimes suddenly a few words that you have really said emerge from
> the past with exactly your voice. (*DPS2*, March 24, 1929; *CJ*, 596–7)

She tells herself that she continues to love him, even after she becomes aware
that he has had a lover, 'Magda', whom he abandoned and whom she meets up
with, consoling herself that Jacques could not have felt the same love for this
woman as he felt for her (*MD*, 315–16). Yet, although she does not admit it to
herself, it is likely as a result of this discovery that by the summer of 1929 she
has begun to transfer her affection from Jacques to the married René Maheu,
whom she calls 'Herbaud' in her published autobiography and 'Lama' in the
diaries, and who invents for her the nickname that Sartre will soon be using,
'Castor' (French for 'beaver') (*MD*, 310–14, 321–5; Kirkpatrick, 2019, 85–93).
Maheu's friendship with Sartre then leads to her intense intellectual and mar-
ginally erotic relationship with the latter, who will exercise an enormous
influence on the rest of her life, while she will have a reciprocally important
impact on him. Initially, she felt intellectually dominated by him, yet, at the
same time, it is clear that her own intellectual self-confidence demanded a lover
who could match or exceed her (*MD*, 343–4).

In the 1979 interview conducted by Margaret Simons and Jessica Benjamin,
Beauvoir rather upsets them by insisting that she was a writer, not a philosopher.
She was as much drawn to literature as to philosophy, and, though she under-
plays its significance, her first love for Jacques and the literary culture she
imbibed while committed to him continues to influence her outlook throughout
her career as a novelist. After meeting Sartre, her philosophical attitudes will
change, but her love for literature and her early sentiments continue to bubble
below the surface. She will attempt to fuse the literary and philosophical sides of
her background by writing novels in which dry philosophical theory engages
with rich concrete experience, as she explains in the article *Literature and
Metaphysics*, in which she defends the philosophical novel, arguing that it
'provides a disclosure of existence in a way unequalled by any other mode of
expression' (*LitM*, 1165; *LitMe*, 276). In emphasising her literary vocation and
modestly declining to be considered a philosopher, Beauvoir suggests that to be
a philosopher one has to build a great system; it is not enough to simply love or
apply philosophical ideas (Benjamin & Simons, 1999, 11). This implies that she
did not see herself as having built a philosophical system. However, in this
account of her ideas, I propose that in fact, during the war, she did construct

a system as a result of her close reading of Hegel. The somewhat confused ideas that she had cobbled together concerning self and other during her university years then developed into a precise schematism, which began to emerge in the structure of her novels and which she elaborated in her more theoretical works, *The Ethics of Ambiguity* and *The Second Sex*.

During the decade from 1929 to 1939, which separated their joint success in coming first (Sartre) and second (Beauvoir) in the *agrégation* and the beginning of the Second World War, both Beauvoir and Sartre would be employed as philosophy teachers, first separately, Beauvoir in Marseilles and Sartre in Le Havre, and then reunited, Beauvoir initially moving to Rouen and later both finding work in Paris. Sartre would publish his first novel, *Nausea* (1938), and a number of philosophical works, which laid the groundwork for the first parts of *Being and Nothingness*. Beauvoir's first attempt at literature, a collection of short stories, *Quand prime le spirituel*, was initially not accepted for publication and only appeared in 1979, and translated into English as, *When Things of the Spirit Come First* in 1982 (*QS*; *WS*). This early work demonstrates many of the preoccupations that had exercised her in the years prior to her relationship with Sartre, but it lacks the clear philosophical articulation that was to result from the fusion of his influence with that of Hegel. The stories build on her experiences as a student and as a young lycée teacher in provincial France. One is a fictionalised account of Zaza's relationship with Merleau-Ponty, called 'Pradelle' in the autobiography, and her tragic death from meningitis (*WS*, 119–66; *MD*, 349–60). The philosophies that had influenced her during this period are evoked. 'Marcelle', for instance, 'gazed despairingly at that stranger's body within which a soul was hidden, precious and inaccessible' (*WS*, 25), while Beauvoir evokes Bergson when 'Chantal' muses that 'dissecting our fleeting expressions, shutting them up in words, and turning them into thoughts very often means coarsely destroying the impalpable shimmer that gives them all their value' (*WS*, 55). But Beauvoir had not yet found a way to successfully integrate her philosophical ideas into her fiction. She would not achieve this until 1943, when she published *L'Invitée*, translated as *She Came to Stay* (*Inv*; *CS*).

2 Sartre and the Discovery of Hegel

Beauvoir's relationship with Sartre had a profound effect on her philosophy, but she also played an enormous part in the development of his ideas. Working on Hegel's philosophy during the first year of the war, while Sartre was first a soldier, then a prisoner of war, and so absent from Paris, Beauvoir wrote that she worked in his name as much as in her own (*WD*, 320). This results in elements of his published work that owe a great deal to her. Revisionist interpretations of their philosophical relationship, published since the 1990s, have moved away from representing her as simply Sartre's disciple, and this is to be applauded; however, some have gone too far in the direction of denying his originality and influence on her, emphasising her impact on him, or the influence on her of other thinkers, to the exclusion of giving him credit for important aspects of the philosophy they jointly developed (Barnes, 1998–9; Fullbrook & Fullbrook, 1993; Kirkpatrick, 2019; Kruks, 1991; Simons, 1997). As a recent discussion of their relationship observes, 'their intellectual development unfolds as a complex dialogue' (Daigle, 2017, 260). Beauvoir had been exposed to similar philosophical trends before meeting Sartre. She had been trained in the same tradition as he, and many of their shared preoccupations were derived from common sources, in particular Alain, Bergson, and Nietzsche (Sartre, 2012, xv; *FA,* 23–5; *PL,* 16–18). But once their relationship had matured, Beauvoir would adopt much of Sartre's vocabulary, in particular the contingency of being and his notion that consciousness introduces nothingness into the heart of being, which without consciousness (being-for-itself) would be an undifferentiated plenitude (being-in-itself). This is related to his claim that it is by virtue of introducing negativity (nothingness) into the heart of being that humanity is not determined but is free. These ideas are intimately linked with the existentialist doctrine that the existence of human consciousness precedes any human essence. We can be conscious of laws that determine how things will act, but, in being conscious of some such law, we transcend it, for we are different from (we transcend) the thing of which we are conscious. So, Sartre concludes, while we can be conscious of laws, there can be no law of consciousness, no essence that constrains what we can become, since we constantly transcend what simply is, towards what is not (Sartre, 1993, Introduction, §3, xxxi–xxxii).

This language and orientation are particularly evident in Beauvoir's earliest published philosophical essay, *Pyrrhus and Cinéas*, grounded in the question, what is worth pursuing (*PC*)? This is also the theme of her second novel, *The Blood of Others*. It is a question that became urgent for a generation that had given up the security of traditional answers offered by family, status, and religion and had then been faced with the rise of Fascism and the Second World War. Beauvoir agrees with Camus's alienated outsider that 'all those ties that others want to impose on him from the outside' are without value (*PCe*, 92). She, like Sartre, insists that it is only by making some goal one's own that it becomes worth pursuing. Value derives from the human capacity to pursue ends, to transcend what is in the light of some objective, and this is a constant surging forward, a transcendence of what is and what has been, towards a chosen future. Those who claim that they act because God wills it or because they are determined by objective values existing in the world outside them are lying to themselves, since they choose to believe in God or the objectivity of the values that they allow to guide their actions. Ultimately, it is up to the individual to distinguish the false from the true God (*PCe*, 102–5).

In this essay, written during 1943 and published in the following year, she, like Sartre, denies that the other can rob us of our freedom. 'The automobile and the airplane change nothing about our freedom, and the slave's chains change nothing about it either' (*PCe*, 124). She distinguishes the freedom intended here, the freedom to resign oneself to slavery or to revolt, from power. The freedom in question is metaphysical, not practical. Noting the close correlation between Sartre's and Beauvoir's views at this juncture, Sonia Kruks deems this essay to be 'too closely aligned with the idealism and voluntarism of Sartre's early ontology' and suggests that, nevertheless, Beauvoir goes beyond Sartre in distinguishing metaphysical freedom from practical power, an interpretation also adopted by Ursula Tidd (Kruks, 2012, 12–13; Tidd, 2004, 34). But it is unfair to Sartre to deem him an idealist. As we have seen, Beauvoir was herself tempted by idealism before she met Sartre, while, from his earliest published works, he rejected idealism. In *L'Imagination* (1936) and *L'Imaginaire* (1940), both grounded in his thesis, Sartre had developed a theory of the difference between perception and imagination that insisted that both, as states of intentional consciousness, are experienced as directed towards objects existing in the real world. Idealism makes the chair I perceive an idea existing in my consciousness, but Sartre objects that it is 'absurd to say the chair is in my perception' (Sartre, 2004, 6–7). In perceiving, we are conscious of what exists outside us. But consciousness can also be directed towards things that do not exist in the present, immediately perceptible, world. Imaginary objects and images of absent things bring with them this element of non-being, nothingness, which, according to Sartre, grounds our freedom. In the introduction to *Being and Nothingness*, he argues, further, that idealism collapses, for if one claims that only ideas exist, then once one asks about the nature of the existence of the being that has those ideas, one is faced with an impasse. Either this being is itself an idea, and one is left with an evanescent set of immaterial Russian dolls – ideas containing ideas, containing ideas – or one must admit that something exists beyond ideas. Berkeley's idealism is supported by the real existence of God and spirit, but without God, idealism collapses. The ideas that come to us from the world we perceive are clearly not within our control; their source exists independently of us, and so we can conclude that being is something that transcends our minds – it exists in itself and does not depend on us (Sartre, 1993, Introduction, §§3–6). However, since it is what it is in-itself and cannot point beyond itself, contingent being is valueless. It is only consciousness – being in the form of being conscious of being – that introduces the nothingness that transcends what merely is and can introduce value and purpose into existence (Sartre, 1943, II.1.i, 109; 1993, 73).

Just as it is a mistake to attribute idealism to Sartre, so too it is a mistake to imply that he fails to distinguish metaphysical freedom from practical power. As Beauvoir insists, when she defends Sartre against a similar critique to Kruks's, developed by Merleau-Ponty, Sartre in *Being and Nothingness* speaks of both freedom and facticity; of the imperative to choose and the material, social, and objective reality that constrains action and limits our power (*PolW*, 206–57). Often, we are free merely in relation to the attitude that we take to an objectively existing situation, but this does not imply that we are fully determined by that situation. These are ideas that Beauvoir and Sartre share at this period and that are at least partly original to him, though they also derive from a shared influence, that of Heidegger.

It is difficult to determine to what extent Beauvoir engaged with Heidegger independently of Sartre, for this question has only rarely been raised (Lundgren-Gothlin, 2003). A good deal of Sartre's *Being and Nothingness* uses but transforms Heidegger's philosophy, in particular his speaking of nothingness. For both, the apprehension of nothingness is connected to anxiety (Heidegger, 1968, 60; Sartre, 1943, I.1.v, 64; 1993, 29). For Heidegger, nothing is the transphenomenal ground of being, while for Sartre, it is curled in the heart of being (Heidegger, 1968, 62). Heidegger attempts to escape the traditional Platonic and Cartesian philosophical stance, according to which thinking is a technique that works on a kind of being distinct from it, while Sartre remains within the Cartesian tradition but rejects substance dualism, attempting to distinguish consciousness from being-in-itself by making it no more than being's internal negation. He accuses Heidegger, in so far as he deprives *Dasein* of the features of con-sciousness, of turning human reality into a blind thing-like being, arguing that, in so far as human reality involves an ecstatic projection of the self, this must be a conscious projection (Sartre, 1943, II.1.i, 109–10; 1993, 73–4). Yet the language both he and Beauvoir use is often Heideggerian; in particular, their term 'realité-humaine' is one that is taken over from the French trans-lation of some of his works, which first appeared in 1938 (Heidegger, 1968, 14). So, on his own account and through their joint appropriation of Heideggerian terms, Sartre influenced Beauvoir. But this is not to say that he was not also influenced by her.

Beauvoir's major impact on him derives from her reading of Hegel. This results in the introduction, into an ontology that originally encompassed only being-in-itself (phenomenal being that is perceived) and being-for-itself (self-conscious being that perceives), a third ontological moment, being-for-others (consciousness of the self as an object existing for the other) (Green & Roffey, 2008; 2010; Sartre, 1993, III.i, 221–302). From July 1940 until January 1941, Beauvoir was studying and thinking about Hegel's *Phenomenology of Spirit*, using it to set up an opposition between a universal and an individual point of view. Initially, she reports finding the Hegelian idea of the unfolding of history consoling. The war overwhelmed her, presenting a moment in a universal history in which the individual is impotently swept up (*WD*, 304). Her fictional character, Jean Blomart, experiences this in *The Blood of Others*: 'war existed … my thoughts, my desires, were no longer anything more than evanescent bubbles which vanished without leaving their mark on the world, without weighing on my soul' (*SA*, 203; *BO*, 158–9). By the end of the year, however, she had moved on from Hegel's 'historical infinity' and rediscovered a place for the individual in her world view (*WD*, 319). Now what she takes from Hegel is a possible foundation for 'a social view of the world' grounded in the mutual recognition of consciousnesses. In it, the only absolute will be 'human consciousness'. She suggests that the existentialist idea 'that human reality (realité-humaine) *is* nothing other than what it *makes itself* be, that toward which it transcends itself' can be combined with 'the exigency of *mutual recognition* of consciousnesses' in order to provide an existentialist humanism that is more satisfactory than Sartre's anti-humanism, as expressed in *Nausea* (*WD*, 319–20). The metaphysical doctrine of human freedom thus nurtures the political doctrine that society should be governed by the mutual recognition of the freedom of consciousnesses. But Hegel also offers the germ of an account of why this is so difficult to achieve.

The Hegel to whom she was introduced at this period was that of Jean Hyppolite's recent French translation of *The Phenomenology of Spirit* and Jean Wahl's *Le malheur de la conscience dans la philosophie de Hegel* (1929). Wahl emphasises the theological and romantic aspects of Hegel's thought: 'One motif runs from the beginning to the end of his thought, that of division, of sin, of pain and little by little it transforms into that of reconciliation and blessedness' (Wahl, 1951, 14). This motif, so reminiscent of themes found in Beauvoir's early diaries, must have drawn her to Hegel, and she was able to extract from his *Phenomenology* a much clearer formulation of the relationship of self to other than that found in these youthful musings. Central to this formulation is a reading of sections of the *Phenomenology of Spirit* devoted to self-consciousness, in particular that on the master and slave or 'lordship and bondage' and the treatment of stoicism, scepticism, and the unhappy consciousness (Hegel, 1977, §§166–230, 104–38). It is perhaps worth noting that Hegel distinguishes perceptual consciousness from full self-consciousness more clearly than Sartre does. According to Sartre, consciousness is already consciousness through and through (Sartre, 1993, xxxi). Even when it is pre-reflective, it has within it a capacity to be reflective, and so brings with it self-consciousness. This constitutes a problem for Sartre's overall metaphysics, since animals plausibly have perceptual consciousness, but they are not metaphysically free. This is a significant failure, since, according to Sartre, consciousness brings with it freedom. Hegel, on the other hand, distinguishes the kind of perceptual consciousness that we share with animals from the sophisticated self-consciousness that we have as humans. Beauvoir does not initially mark this difference that exists between Sartre and Hegel, but instead develops a modified Hegelianism incorporating Sartrean assumptions. For Sartre, since consciousness is always consciousness of something other than consciousness – an object of consciousness that exists outside it – what we identify as the self is actually an ego, an imaginary object with which we identify. For Hegel, self-consciousness exists and can know itself, a position that Sartre rejects (Sartre, 1993, III.i.3, 235–44).

Hegel begins from a rather different place to Sartre, but one that is nevertheless compatible with the Sartrean idea of consciousness as the negation of being-in-itself. Self-consciousness, according to Hegel, begins as '*Desire* in general' (Hegel, 1977, §166, 105). Consciousness as self-consciousness is not just passive consciousness of perceptual objects, which are different from the conscious being, but is consciousness of the self's desire for the perceived objects, in particular as objects that the self lacks and desires to consume. As a living thing, 'being *for itself* . . . comes forward in antithesis to the universal substance . . . [and] preserves itself by separating itself from this inorganic nature, and by consuming it' (Hegel, 1977, §171, 107). Self-consciousness, as life, described by Hegel in the subsequent sections, is very close to Sartrean consciousness, it is 'simple being-for-itself, self-equal through the exclusion from itself of everything else' (Hegel, 1977, §186, 113). Other self-conscious beings (if they exist) do not exist for this self-consciousness as self-consciousnesses, but only as objects of consciousness. One could call this the state of solipsistic self-consciousness, the state that had initially attracted Beauvoir. For Hegel, this is a kind of unconscious self-consciousness, for he claims that it is only when a self-consciousness exists for another self-consciousness that 'the unity of itself in its otherness' becomes explicit for it (Hegel, 1977, §177, 110). He promises a higher self-consciousness, which is, the experience of what Spirit is – this absolute substance which is the unity of the different independent self-consciousnesses which in their opposition, enjoy perfect freedom and independence: 'I' that is 'We' and 'We' that is 'I'. It is in self-consciousness, in the Notion of Spirit, that consciousness first finds its turning point, where it leaves behind the colourful show of the sensuous here-and-now and the nightlike void of the supersensible beyond, and steps out into the spiritual daylight of the present. (Hegel, 1977, §177, 110–11)

For Beauvoir and for Sartre, this resolution of the separation of self-consciousnesses in Absolute Spirit is a consoling myth. Consciousness, being mere negation of being-in-itself, is self-conscious but cannot be conscious of another consciousness. To be conscious of something is to be conscious of it as an object. So, although Beauvoir will adapt ideas, which for Hegel are steps on the path to the mutual recognition of self-consciousnesses, both she and Sartre will retain in their philosophies elements of the unbroachable separation of consciousnesses, which is the legacy of the Cartesian origins of their philosophy.

In the influential passages on lordship and bondage that follow his description of self-consciousness as desire, Hegel sees himself as tracing steps that will progress towards the unity of the I and the We. For Beauvoir, and even more clearly for Sartre, the forms of self-consciousness that he describes in these passages become two ineluctable moments in the human experience of the self, between which we ambiguously vacillate but which we can never completely transcend. Beginning from the solipsistic, individual, self-consciousness that is simple being-for-itself, Hegel describes the other self-consciousness as like an ordinary object (Hegel, 1977, §186, 113). At this point Hegel claims that for the truth of an individual's self-consciousness to be objectively recognised, the self-consciousness of the other must also be recognised. He then introduces the rather strange idea that it is out of a life and death struggle, in which one consciousness seeks the death of the other, that the aggressor consciousness also stakes its life and so, in a sense, recognises the truth of its own self-consciousness as a living thing (Hegel, 1977, §187, 113–14). 'Life is as essential to it as pure self-consciousness' (Hegel, 1977, §189, 115). But the death of the adversary robs the victor of this external recognition of the truth of its self-consciousness. It is only in submitting, suing for life and accepting slavery, rather than death, that the simple unity of self-consciousness transforms into two 'essential moments':

One is the independent consciousness whose essential nature is to be for itself, the other is the dependent consciousness whose essential nature is simply to live or to be for another. The former is lord, the other is bondsman. (Hegel, 1977, §189, 115)

These two moments of self-consciousness will be put to use by Beauvoir in order to account for the situation of women. But before adapting them as the basis for her broad sociological thesis, she used them to structure her account of a series of fractured personal relationships in her first published novel, *She Came to Stay* (*Inv*;*CS*).

As with her earlier suite of stories, this novel is grounded in her own experience, a triangular relationship that developed between Sartre, Beauvoir, and Olga Kosakievicz, while Beauvoir was teaching at Rouen, where Olga was a student. This was to develop into a four way relationship once Jacques-Laurent Bost entered the scene (Kirkpatrick 2019, 137–60). The novel opens with Françoise walking through a darkened theatre. Things jump into existence as she sees them: 'when she was not there, the smell of dust, the half-light, and their forlorn solitude did not exist for anyone; they did not exist at all' (*CS*, 1). She lives in a solipsistic universe in which she 'wants to be everything' (*FCh*, I.92; *FC*, 70–1). Françoise loves Pierre, feeling secure in herself as a result of this love, but this naïve solipsism is destroyed by the appearance of Xavière. At first, Françoise treats her with indifference, but as she begins to impose her own point of view on things, her judgements cannot be ignored. By the end of the third chapter of part one, Françoise cannot deny Xavière's concrete existence; by the end of the fourth chapter of part two, she finds the recognition of this independent consciousness intolerable (*CS*, 61, 296–7). As a relationship between Xavière and Pierre begins to develop, Françoise becomes insecure; realising that she has become dependent on him, she attempts to retain her independence (*CS*, 108–9). Indeed, it seems that she is able to avenge herself against Xavière, not only by retaining Pierre's love, but also by stealing from her Gerbert, with whom Xavière has begun a new relationship. But her duplicity is discovered, and unable to face the harsh judgement that she knows that she well deserves, Françoise retains her dominance by turning on the gas and killing Xavière in an act of destructive hate (*CS*, 402–9).

In an early analysis of this novel, Hazel Barnes showed how well the various attitudes expressed by these characters map onto the description of concrete relations with others, as described in *Being and Nothingness* (Barnes, 1959). But rather than simply being an application of Sartre's philosophy, as Barnes assumed, we should see the schema applied there by Beauvoir, and also developed by Sartre, as grounded in her reading of Hegel. Hegel's 'independent consciousness whose essential nature is to be for itself', the consciousness of the master, becomes Sartre's freedom that confronts the Other and makes it 'a transcendence transcended', as expressed in indifference, desire, sadism, and hate (Sartre, 1993, III.iii.2, 379), while Hegel's slave consciousness, 'the dependent consciousness whose essential nature is simply to live or to be for another', becomes an attitude to the Other in which 'I make the Other the foundation of my being' expressed in love, language, and masochism (Sartre, 1993, III.iii.1, 364–5). Françoise exemplifies both forms of consciousness: she is the dependent consciousness in relation to Pierre, but in her relation to Xavière, both in her first indifference and later in her destructive act of hate, she attempts to transcend the other's transcendence. At the same time, there are elements in the novel that are not found in Sartre's adaptation of Hegel; in particular, the characterisation of love, as Françoise initially imagines it, as the unification of the consciousnesses of the lovers, does not correspond to anything found in Sartre's *Being and Nothingness*.

The way that Beauvoir describes the relationship that she developed with Sartre has elements in common with the way in which she represents Françoise's love for Pierre. She and Sartre have so assiduously 'always criticized, corrected or ratified each other's thought that we might almost to be said to think in common' (*FCh*, II.489; *FC*, 659). But she also points out that, although their writings have sprung from a common ground, their temperaments are quite different and their writings 'almost totally dissimilar' (*FCh*, II.490; *FC*, 659). The equal intellectual relationship that she attempted to forge with him has, without her acknowledging it, elements of the Hegelian 'unity of the different independent self-consciousnesses', the I that is We and We that is I. This dream of unity in division appears far more insistently in Beauvoir's writing than in Sartre's, capturing, perhaps, what she imagined to be an authentic love.

In a letter to Sartre written during the war, Beauvoir had said, 'I would so much like us to develop a confrontation of your ideas on nothingness, being in-itself and being for-itself and the ideas of Hegel' (*LS*, 181–2). What emerged in Sartre's work, as a result of this confrontation, was a form of truncated dialectic, in which the two forms of self-consciousness that, for Hegel, emerge out of a life and death struggle, are never transcended but remain forever attitudes that individuals (at least those in bad faith) adopt towards each other. Significant liberties are taken by the existentialists with the Hegelian schema. The conflict assumed is no longer necessarily the result of a life and death struggle but, according to Sartre, emerges from the character of consciousness itself, which, he assumes, tends towards a solipsistic individualism that naturally wants to be sovereign, thus being threatened by the recognition of the existence of an external self-consciousness that promises to transform the conscious subject, experiencing the look of the other, into an object.

Beauvoir had continued the letter to Sartre, quoted above, by explaining that 'Hegel transforms into joy that which is with you more sombre and despairing. And it seems to me that both are true, and I would like to find a point of equilibrium' (*LS*, 182). She was attracted to the possibility of an ethic grounded in some form of mutual recognition, and in her longest philosophical essay, *Pour une morale de l'ambiguité,* translated as *An Ethics of Ambiguity*, she initially sets out to show how the existentialist emphasis on the isolation and separateness of the individual can nevertheless be made compatible with a universal ethic applicable to all (*MA*, 25; *EA*, 18). She is later critical of this essay, for the position it develops is arguably too abstract to be compelling; she condemns it for offering a solution to the ethical problem 'as hollow as the Kantian maxims' (*FCh*, I.99; *FC*, 76). Yet it contains the fullest outline of the existentialist humanism to which she adhered at that time and that she outlined as the joint position of a 'we' that encompassed Sartre. The ambiguity of the title is that of the human condition, of freedom and facticity and of the individual within the collective. For 'the privilege, which [humanity] alone possesses, of being a sovereign and unique subject amidst a universe of objects, is what he shares with all his fellow-men. In turn an object for others, he is nothing more than an individual in the collectivity on which he depends' (*EA*, 7). The principle on which Beauvoir attempts to build an ethic is one of honesty. If we are, as is claimed, meta-physically ambiguous, we should not flee this ambiguity but 'assume' it. But what does this mean? There are two ways in which individuals are tempted to flee their ambiguity: one is to deny their freedom, the other to deny the reality of the situation in which they find themselves. On the moral plane, the first form of bad faith involves fleeing freedom. It is the attitude of Sartre's 'serious' person, who claims that values exist in the external world and determine action, as he describes in *Being and Nothingness*, which Beauvoir calls, 'in large part a description of the serious man and his universe' (*EA*, 46). A serious attitude lies behind many of the most atrocious acts committed by humans, who, by claiming that their acts are necessary in the light of absolute values, absolve themselves from responsibility for their free choices. In the critique of seriousness one can read an analysis of the attitude that made Nazism possible. It is also the attitude of the inquisitor or, more recently, of the Islamic jihadist. Serious individuals appeal to external values, which compel their subjection. Diametrically opposed to this, but in a sense equally mistaken, is the nihilist, who, realising that there are no absolute objective values, concludes that anything is acceptable. This involves the denial of the reality of the situation in which we find ourselves, in which acts have conse-quences for other people: 'the nihilist is a systematic rejection of the world and man' (*EA*, 57). One can characterise these two ethical attitudes as correspond-ing to dogmatism and scepticism more generally, and in attempting to formu-late what she takes to be an authentic ethical attitude, Beauvoir employs an ethical correlate of Husserl's *epoché*, the suspension of belief that he recommends as a means of moving from scepticism to well-grounded belief. In the ethical sphere, this involves a 'conversion',

> just as phenomenological reduction prevents the errors of dogmatism by suspending all affirmation concerning the mode of reality of the external world, whose flesh and bone presence the reduction does not, however, contest, so existentialist conversion does not suppress my instincts, desires, plans, and passions. It merely prevents any possibility of failure by refusing to set up as absolutes the ends toward which my transcendence thrusts itself, and by considering them in their connection with the freedom which projects them. (*EA*, 14)

Sartre will also explore the possibility of such an ethical 'conversion' in his *Notebooks for an Ethics* and will conclude that one cannot be converted alone (Sartre, 1992). In 1946, Beauvoir apparently considers it to be an attitude that individuals can and ought to freely adopt, though later in the essay, when she discusses the concept of oppression, she comments, 'for a liberating action to be a thoroughly moral action, it would have to be achieved through a conversion of the oppressors: there would then be a reconciliation of all freedoms. But no one any longer dares to abandon himself today to these utopian reveries' (*EA*, 96–7). Since she also claims that the oppressed find themselves in situations in which there is no real possibility of adopting an authentic attitude, it becomes difficult to conceive in what kind of situation authenticity is possible.

One might, nevertheless, find in Beauvoir's description of this 'conversion' an undertheorised divergence from Sartre. In his *Sketch for a Theory of Emotions*, he had treated emotional states as forms of play acting, suggesting that we choose to be sad, angry, or offended (Sartre, 1939; 1962). Counterintuitively, he suggests we are free, even in what we feel. Beauvoir is far more attuned to the way in which emotion wells up and takes us over, as she has a novelist's appreciation of the phenomenology of emotion. Thus, in the quoted passage, she does not deny the reality of instincts, desires, and passions, nor assume that we can choose what we feel. Rather, our freedom and capacity for authenticity consists in the ability to disengage from our emotional impulses – just as Husserl claims we can suspend belief in the apparent objectivity of perception – so as to more thoroughly ground them. In her novels and works on women and ageing, what one is made to feel about oneself by others, its emotional resonance, is an important aspect of the way in which not all situations are equal in regard to freedom.

The war had united different groups in France in opposition to Nazism, but with the liberation they had begun to disagree over the direction that left-wing politics should take. Written at this moment of history, *The Ethics of*

Ambiguity offers the first steps of an existentialist engagement with Marxism, which will come to dominate Beauvoir and Sartre's attention in the coming years. Beauvoir represents the Marxists as similar to the existentialists in regarding value as the creation of humanity but as differing from them in so far as they insist that what humans desire is not a free expression of the will. Rather, for them, what is willed is 'the reflection of objective conditions by which the situation of the class or the people under consideration is defined' (*EA*, 19). The issue of individual freedom 'is the essential point on which existentialist ontology is opposed to dialectical materialism' (*EA*, 20). Yet at the same time Beauvoir begins to utilise concepts of class, race, and oppression borrowed from Marxism and other movements of liberation, which sit rather uneasily with the existentialist emphasis on metaphysical liberty. She is not unaware of this tension, so one way of reading the *Ethics of Ambiguity* is as an attempt to deal with certain limitations of Sartre's existentialism, both as found in his early writing and as it had developed out of the confrontation of that early philosophy with Hegel's theories. Three related issues arise. First, if freedom is a metaphysical characteristic that cannot be lost, how can one will to be free? Second, since children are conscious, should they not also be considered free and responsible? But we don't consider them to be morally responsible. And third, if we are metaphysically free, how can one account for oppression, characterised as the loss of freedom? In another author's hands, these questions might be developed into devastating critiques of Sartre's metaphysics of consciousness and freedom, but Beauvoir attempts to offer a reconciliation of the tensions involved, though, arguably, they continue to reverberate throughout her subsequent writings, as well as in the reception of her philosophy.

The answer to the first of these questions has already been indicated. While there is justice in the remark that 'It is contradictory to set freedom up as something conquered if at first it is something given', it is also the case that individuals are tempted to deny their freedom. 'One can choose not to will oneself free. In laziness, heedlessness, capriciousness, cowardice, impatience, one contests the meaning of the project at the very moment that one defines it' (*EA*, 25). Beauvoir's answer to the second question attempts to flesh out how a situation in which one denies one's freedom can arise. The child exists in a world in which values are given, they form the structure of the child's world, and they cannot be chosen (*EA*, 35). It is only as it matures that a child comes to see itself as a temporal entity, with a past and a future, and in recognising its temporality it is faced with the imperative to create a future for itself. Then it is forced to either accept or question the values that surround it, so two options open up: one is to accept that it is free and responsible, in so far as it chooses to adopt or reject the given values; the other is to fail to acknowledge this freedom, to flee the responsibilities of adulthood, and to mire itself in one of the inauthentic attitudes that Beauvoir goes on to describe. In effect, Beauvoir here introduces a distinction between metaphysical and moral freedom, which appears to be at odds with Sartre's identification of freedom with consciousness. Alternatively, she can be read as introducing a clarification, which makes explicit an element of his theory glossed over by Sartre, that saves his account from the objection raised earlier, that since animals and children are conscious, they ought, on his account, to be free. It is clear that the negativity that consciousness brings with it, according to Sartre, is bound up with temporality; that is, the capacity of consciousness to think of a time that is not yet, that is no longer, or that has never been. Arguably, animals and children, although they have perceptual consciousness, lack a fully developed temporal consciousness of this kind, which would allow them to transcend the present moment and project themselves into the future, or in imagination into various possible futures.[2] It is only this kind of full temporal self-consciousness that brings with it freedom, and this is something that children develop but also something that humans can deny when they choose not to recognise that various options are available to them. Beauvoir's understanding of conscious transcendence thus has Heideggerian as well as Hegelian roots, since it is the former who insists on the temporal structure of human reality as the opening up of possibilities or the revealing of being.

This elaboration, or modification, of the notion of consciousness allows Beauvoir to introduce the idea that not all situations are equally compatible with the exercise of freedom, and so to offer an account of oppression. There are some situations in which alternative possibilities do not present themselves. Beauvoir suggests that women, who were historically confined to a harem, and southern slaves were enclosed in such a situation (*EA*, 38). Not only were different possible futures physically closed off to them, but even the possibility of imagining an alternative future was unavailable. Although she does not mention them, laws prohibiting slaves from learning to read and traditions that refuse education to women fit well into this account of the nature of oppression, for such laws are intended to prevent the

---

[2] The idea that animal consciousness is completely atemporal may well be contested, since animals, for instance squirrels, apparently plan for the future and remember the past, so it can't be claimed that animals have no sense of themselves as temporal beings. Freedom, however, does seem to be intimately connected with the capacity to imagine various non-existent possible futures, and this kind of temporal consciousness does appear to be necessary and possibly sufficient for moral freedom and responsibility.

oppressed from being able to imagine alternative futures or to formulate choices, restricting their lives to present experience and confining them to a world, the shape of which is determined by others. Oppression is then characterised as the closing off of possible futures by other humans. And since it is possible for others to oppress us, and given that, as authentic free individuals, we will wish to pursue the values and futures we have chosen, consistency will require that we support the freedom of all.

> My freedom, in order to fulfil itself, requires that it emerge into an open future: it is other men who open the future to me, it is they who, setting up the world of tomorrow, define my future; but if, instead of allowing me to participate in this constructive movement, they oblige me to consume my transcendence in vain, if they keep me below the level which they have conquered and on the basis of which new conquests will be achieved then they are cutting me off from the future, they are changing me into a thing. (*EA*, 82)

Since my freedom depends on how I am treated by others, I should promote the freedom of others. This is the prescriptive injunction that Beauvoir attempts to derive from the description of humanity as metaphysically free. The ethical position that emerges is therefore 'at one with the point of view of Christian charity, the Epicurean cult of friendship, and Kantian moralism which treats each man as an end' (*EA*, 135). But, as Beauvoir comments later, the existentialist ethic that emerges, which involves making freedom the absolute value, is hollow, for it offers no guidance with regard to the conflicts that inevitably arise between individual freedoms over the values to be pursued.

Having developed the position that there are oppressed groups, for whose members the failure to adopt an authentic attitude is not a moral failure, mired in bad faith, but is the result of oppression, Beauvoir moves on to discuss the antinomies of action. Given the situation in which the oppressed find themselves, she suggests that there is no option open to them but to revolt, but the aim of such a revolt is to constrain the freedom of the oppressors.

> However, by virtue of the fact that the oppressors refuse to co-operate in the affirmation of freedom, they embody, in the eyes of all men of good will, the absurdity of facticity; by calling for the triumph of freedom over facticity, ethics also demands that they be suppressed; and since their subjectivity, by definition, escapes our control, it will be possible to act only on their objective presence; others will here have to be treated like things, with violence; the sad fact of the separation of men will thereby be confirmed. (*EA*, 97)

This paradox is so deep that it seems impossible to resolve. If freedom is understood in a libertarian manner, as an uncaused upwelling that creates value through individual choice, while at the same time it is claimed that certain social situations can stifle freedom, it becomes almost impossible to imagine how to solve such antimonies of action. Actually, if members of an oppressed class are sufficiently aware of their oppression to be able to revolt, they must have attained the kind of temporal self-consciousness that posits a different future, and so to that extent be free. Yet, if this is so, their desire to limit the freedom of the privileged appears morally on a par with the oppressor's desire to limit their freedom. It is only by appeal to some sort of principle of justice, for instance, the idea that what is fair is that there should be the greatest extent of liberty compatible with a like liberty for all, that unjustified incursions into the freedom of others could be distinguished from legitimate claims. Yet, to set up a principle such as this as absolute would, from the existentialist point of view, be to fall back into the spirit of seriousness.

Ultimately, Beauvoir allows that this is a paradox that cannot be resolved. Since individuals have conflicting projects, 'if division and violence define war, the world has always been at war and always will be; if man is waiting for universal peace in order to establish his existence validly, he will wait indefinitely: there will never be any *other* future' (*EA*, 119). Nevertheless, since society is made up of individuals and the values that individuals adhere to are values for all that point beyond themselves towards an open future, value systems that fail to recognise the role that others play in their adoption are doomed to fail. If other consciousnesses fail to endorse the projects we choose, then our goals will die with us. No matter what the project, 'the practical attitude remains the same; we must decide upon the opportuneness of an act and attempt to measure its effectiveness without knowing all the factors that are present' (*EA*, 123). But since it is a paradox that cannot be resolved, just as the ambiguity of freedom and facticity cannot be resolved, it is a tension that has to be faced up to.

> In order for the return to the positive to be genuine, it must involve negativity, it must not conceal the antinomies between means and end, present and future; they must be lived in a permanent tension; one must retreat from neither the outrage of violence nor deny it, or, which amounts to the same thing, assume it lightly. (*EA*, 133)

On the practical plane, then, the moral individual who has been converted from bad faith to authenticity will pursue their beliefs and values without giving up doubt. They will continue to question, asking, 'Am I really working for the liberation of men? Isn't this end contested by the sacrifices through which I aim at it?' Or, as Beauvoir explains in more philosophical terms, 'In setting up its ends, freedom must put them in parentheses, confront them at each moment with that absolute end which it itself constitutes, and contest, in its own name, the means it uses to win itself' (*EA*, 133–4). Whether such an attitude can prevail against dogmatic certitude or cynical nihilism is a question that she fails to consider.

So, although at the beginning of this essay Beauvoir had claimed that 'An ethics of ambiguity will be one which will refuse to deny *a priori* that separate existents can, at the same time, be bound to each other, that their individual freedoms can forge laws valid for all', by the end she has renounced the project of 'forging laws valid for all', offering instead the vision of the necessity of commitment to finite ends that make sense from a particular concrete point of view but that are bound to be contested by others. Taking the freedom of others seriously does not end up involving the mutual recognition of self-consciousnesses so much as the acceptance of the inevitability of conflict among consciousnesses, of which it is assumed, following Descartes, that their 'subjectivity radically signifies separation' (*EA*, 105). The existentialist adaptation of Hegel, which one finds also in Fanon, here points in the direction of a Manichaean, violent struggle, without any clear prospects for resolution (Green, 1999; Stawarska, 2020).

Three years separated the publication of *The Ethics of Ambiguity* from that of *The Second Sex*. During these years, Beauvoir visited America, became involved with the writer Nelson Algren, and published *America Day by Day* (*ADD*): an account of her rather unfavourable impressions of American chauvinism, racism, consumerism, and intellectual shallowness. While there, her introduction to US culture was partly guided by the black writer Richard Wright and his wife Ellen, whom she already knew from Paris, and she was encouraged by them to read *An American Dilemma*, which had been based on research by the Swede Gunner Myrdal (1944). Reading it convinced her that she should broaden the scope of the essay on women that she had begun publishing in *Les Temps Modernes* and that would become *The Second Sex* (Simons, 1999, 170–1; *FM*). It also confirmed her in the view that there were analogies between racism and sexism. Myrdal comments that the 'negro' can only speak as a 'negro', 'he would seem entirely out of place if he spoke simply as a . . . citizen of America or as a man of the world' (Myrdal, 1944, 18). Similarly, Beauvoir points out that men can speak for the universal, while, when a woman speaks, she is taken to speak as a woman: 'man represents both the positive and the neuter' (*DS*, I.Intro, 14; *SSp*,15; *SSbm*, 5). Myrdal examines 'the negro question' from a sociological point of view and takes racial difference to be socially constructed. *The Second Sex* has been read, similarly, as a sociological account of the situation of women, but reading it in this way minimises its phenomenological and existentialist under-pinnings. In the following chapter, it will be analysed in the light of the philo-sophical schemata developed in *The Ethics of Ambiguity* applied, extended, and to an extent transformed in her account of the situation of women, which Beauvoir asserts is written from the perspective of an existentialist ethic (*DS*, I.Intro, 33; *SSp*, 27; *SSbm*, 17).

3 *The Second Sex*

One of the most influential philosophical works of the twentieth century, *The Second Sex* spawned a generation of feminist descendants, whose authors did not always acknowledge its influence and tended to ride rough-shod over its philosophical underpinnings (Dijkstra, 1980). Beauvoir herself is somewhat to blame for this. Although she states in her introduction that the perspective adopted is one of an 'existentialist ethic', she never spells out what this implies (*DS*, I.Intro, 33; *SSp*, 27; *SSbm*, 17). She also adapts and develops ideas from various philosophical, biological, anthropological, and psychoanalytic traditions that are ultimately not clearly compatible with an existentialist outlook. Nevertheless, in this, her most influential work, she put her considerable skills as a writer to use, in order to craft a compelling account of what it was to be a white, middle-class woman during the mid-twentieth century.[3] Its descriptions resonated with many of those who read it, and she furnished subsequent generations of women with a vocabulary and framework that they soon put to use to articulate the situation in which they found themselves.

Central to its impact is Beauvoir's application of Hegel's distinction between the dependant and the independent consciousness to the situation of women and men. Adapting the words of Michelet, Benda, and Levinas, for whom woman is an Other, whose existence is relative to man, Beauvoir asserts of woman,

> She is nothing other than that which man decides; thus, one calls her 'the sex', signifying, in so doing, that she appears to the male essentially as a sexed being; for him she is sex, so that is what she is essentially. She identifies and differentiates herself in relation to men and he does not do so in relation to her; she is the inessential presented with the essential. He is the Subject, he is the Absolute: she is the Other. (*DS*, I.Intro, 17; *SSp*, 16; *SSbm*, 6)[4]

This is a claim that will have an incalculable impact on the development of feminism during the second half of the twentieth century. Yet, from its first articulation, it raises certain questions. In works such as *She Came to Stay*, Beauvoir had assumed that women could be the dominant, essential subject for whom others are objects – this is the attitude that Françoise attempts to maintain in relation to Xavière. Indeed, the account of the ambiguity of the

---

[3] Some women of colour and from other cultures have questioned whether she speaks for them; others have found inspiration in her example (Gines, 2010; Perpich, 2017; Vintges, 2017).

[4] Here and elsewhere, I have modified the available translations.

human condition that she had developed in *The Ethics of Ambiguity* implied that all fully developed humans are both consciousness and matter, both subject and object. But this raises the question, how is it that women don't treat themselves as the Absolute? How is it that men are not made to define and experience themselves in relation to women? In *Ethics of Ambiguity*, Beauvoir had begun to develop the idea that certain social situations prevent the possibility of experiencing oneself as a free transcendent subject, suggesting that this is the situation both for slaves and for some classes of women. *The Second Sex* extends this idea, arguing that the situation in which women find themselves is one that, in some cases, amounts to an oppression that eliminates the possibility of free self-expression, while in others it presents overwhelming temptations that encourage women to fall into the bad faith of denying their freedom (*DS*, I.Intro, 24–5; *SSp*, 20; *SSbm*, 10).

Having introduced the claim that woman is the Other of man, the inessential object in relation to the essential subject, Beauvoir turns to the question of why it is that women have not challenged the situation and made men their Other. In Hegel's dialectic, the slaves rise up, challenging the master's dominance, and a new stage of history is reached, one in which self-consciousnesses recognise themselves collectively in the Absolute Spirit. We have seen that the existentialists reject this Hegelian reconciliation of the separation of consciousnesses. Rather, according to them, the objectified and objectifying attitudes become two forms of consciousness, adopted by people in bad faith, among which individuals vacillate. When Beauvoir had applied this truncated Hegelian schematism to the situation of individuals in her novels, she had assumed that both women and men could adopt both attitudes, but in *The Second Sex* she proposes that certain social situations encourage members of certain groups to remain fixed in a particular attitude, as a result of their relationship with another group. This is what happens in the case of oppression. Beauvoir points to analogies between the situation of women and that of the proletariat under capitalism, of blacks in the USA, and of Jews in Europe. In each of these cases, members of a group find themselves represented, by members of a more powerful collectivity, as Other, as not part of the We who comprise the identity of a people. But, in each of these historical inequalities, the oppressed have more readily come together to challenge their objectification than have women. Beauvoir claims that the situation of women is singular. Whereas these other oppressions can be located at a particular historical moment and 'the opposing groups concerned were once independent of each other', in the case of women, who are identified 'by their physiological structure; as far back as history can be traced, they have always been subordinate to men; their dependence is not the consequence of an event or a becoming, it did not *happen*. It is, in part, because it does not have the accidental character of a historical fact that alterity here appears to be an absolute' (*DS*, I.Intro, 21; *SSp*, 19; *SSbm*, 8).

The situation of women is thus, according to Beauvoir, singular. Women, she claims, 'do not use "we"; men say "women" and women adopt this word to refer to themselves; but they do not posit themselves authentically as Subjects'. She continues,

> Women's actions have never been more than symbolic agitation; they have won only what men have been willing to concede to them; they have taken nothing; they have received. This is because they do not have the concrete means to come together as a unity that could posit itself in opposing itself [to some other]. They have no past, no history, no religion of their own.
>
> (*DS*, I.Intro, 21; *SSp*, 18; *SSbm*, 8)

She continues by emphasising the incomparability of the relationship between men and women with these other historical oppressions by claiming that 'sexual difference is, in effect, a biological given, not a phase of human history' (*DS*, I. Intro, 23; *SSp*, 19; *SSbm*, 9). The opposition between the sexes developed within an original *Mitsein* or totality in which the two halves are riven together and depend on each other. Later, when she gives an account of women's history, she repeats the claim that 'the history of women was created by men' (*DS*, I.2.v, 222; *SSp*, 148; *SSbm*, 150). Men's technological advances have enfranchised contemporary women, who have 'never sought to play a role in history as a sex'. Even feminism itself had 'never been an autonomous movement'; it was merely 'an instrument in the hands of politicians' or 'an epiphenomenon reflecting a deeper social drama' (*DS*, I.2.v, 223; *SSp*, 149; *SSbm*, 151). These rather surprising conclusions are encouraged by influences that are quite alien to the existentialist perspective to which Beauvoir was explicitly committed, in particular, her encounter with Lévi-Strauss's *Elementary Structures of Kinship* (Lévi-Strauss, 1949).

The first results of Beauvoir's exploration of female identity were published in *Les Temps Modernes* as 'Les femmes et les mythes' (*FM*). Already, in these early essays, she had developed the idea that women are the Other of men (*FM*, 1923). In *The Second Sex* this was reinforced by being combined with Lévi-Strauss's claim that women are objects of exchange. As she tells us in her autobiography, she learnt that Lévi-Strauss had criticised aspects of the early essays, and as a result she contacted him and read a draft of his *Elementary Structures* before it was published (*FCh*, I.235; *FC*, 177). Later, she also published a laudatory review of this work, in which she had found confirmation of the claim that 'as far back as history can be traced' women have always been subordinate to men. There, following Lévi-Strauss, she asserts, 'relations of reciprocity and exchange do not appear between men and women; they are established between men *by means of women*. A profound asymmetry between the sexes exists and always has existed' (*RES*, 60–1). She follows him in rejecting the idea that there was an earlier stage of culture in which women were dominant, and she accepts that, whether they are matrilineal or patrilineal, 'All matrimonial systems entail that women are given by certain males to other males' (*RES*, 61). The result encourages a reading of *The Second Sex* according to which to say that women are the inessential, or the Other of man, goes beyond the claim that they are tempted to experience themselves as dependent consciousnesses and implies a reading of women's situation according to which they are merely objects of exchange in cultures that completely depend on men's interests, language, and sexual desires. This results in later developments of the idea that culture is grounded in a contract between men, while woman is the Other of man, that problematise the possibility of any authentic female subjectivity (Irigaray, 1985a; 1985b; Pateman, 1988).

As Beauvoir herself had emphasised in *Pyrrhus and Cinéas*, each individual is thrown into history at a particular moment and pursues their finite projects without any certainty that others will collude in achieving them (*PCe*, 140). This applies as much to her own situation as to any other, and one can question whether, in following Lévi-Strauss so faithfully, she was not blinkered by the limitations of the historical moment in which she found herself. The elite university scholarship into which she had been inducted, during the first half of the twentieth century, assumed that culture had been created by men. Early anthropologists had acted on this assumption and in general confined their questioning of indigenous peoples to elite, older males, to a certain extent by necessity, since, as most of the anthropologists were men, they had little access to the women's sphere in what were generally sex segregated societies. So, men's views of women were recorded by anthropologists, and the theory of the maleness of culture was reinforced by the self-perpetuating method of excluding women from cultural investigation. This tendency was already being challenged during the 1940s by a few women, such as Margaret Mead (1943). Even earlier, Bronislaw Malinowski, whose works Beauvoir knew, had been interested in the extent of women's agency in matrilineal societies (Malinowski, 1937; *DS*, I.3.i, 259; *SSp*, 171; *SSbm*, 177). But it was not until the 1970s that female anthropologists and socio-biologists began to explicitly question the male bias in anthropology and evolutionary history and to engage seriously with female informants, exploring women's own accounts of their participation in cultural activities, taking their estimation of the significance of their role in the maintenance of their culture as authoritative, and theorising them as active competitors for resources in the process of evolution (Bell, 1983; Hrdy, 2000;

Sanday, 1981). These authors begin to describe how women actively participate in the complex structures of reciprocity between skins, generations, and sexes, which meld together indigenous societies, in which each individual participates in a web of complex oppositions between self and other, reciprocity and taboo. They began to propose that women actively engage in competition with men and with other women for resources, and that marriage and kinship systems achieve various kinds of equilibria among male and female interests. However, none of this later, feminist-inspired anthropology was available to Beauvoir.

The questionable objectivity of the male-centred anthropology to which Beauvoir was exposed is a symptom of a more general feature of her historical situation. As a member of a first small cohort of women initiated into what had, up until then, been a completely male-dominated academy, the philosophical works that she was exposed to were all written by men, the culture was male dominated, and the place of women within intellectual history minimised. Although she was aware of the activities of a large number of historical women, in particular poets, authors, and noblewomen, who had been influential from the fifteenth to the eighteenth century, and whose names she catalogues in her sections on history, she does not allow that these women had achieved any significant cultural impact (*DS*, I.2.v, 222–31; *SSp*, 159–68; *SSbm*, 150–9). She mentions Christine de Pizan, whose *Letter of the God of Love* she knew. Yet, she had not read it sufficiently carefully to have noticed that, three hundred years before Poulain de la Barre – whom she quotes with approbation for saying that men's accounts of women are suspect, because men are both judge and party – Christine had already commented that 'men plead their own cases', observing that, had women written books, they would have written them differently (*DS*, I. Intro, 24; *SSp*, 21; *SSbm*, 10–11; Blumenfeld-Kosinski, 1998, 22–3). Beauvoir is well aware of Marguerite of Navarre's *Heptameron*, which she had studied at university, saying of her that she was 'the writer who best served the cause of her sex', but, as with other works by women, she does not attribute to it any significant impact, though it could be argued that its expropriation of Platonic ideas, in order to elevate the status of married love, made a decisive step in the direction of establishing women's image as men's spiritual equals and encouraged the development of conjugal marriage (*MD*, 171; *DS*, I.2.iv, 185; *SSp*, 129; *SSbm*, 125). Beauvoir knows the history of the women's suffrage movement, yet, in the end, she sums up her account of women's history with the assessment that 'a few isolated individuals – Sappho, Christine de Pizan, Mary Wollstonecraft, Olympe de Gouges – protested the harshness of their fate', but 'when they intervened in world affairs, it was in concert with men and from a masculine point of view' (*DS*, I.2.v, 222–3; *SSp*, 148–9; *SSbm*, 150–1). Here, the historical moment in which she wrote and the application of the modified

Hegelian schematism that she applied prevented Beauvoir from taking seriously the ample evidence of past women's striving for, and, to a certain extent, achievement of, transcendence. Indeed, ironically, the accusation of writing from a masculine point of view would, in turn, soon be levelled against her by feminists who had concluded, on the basis of the diffusion of her own schematism, that to pursue transcendence was, inherently, to adopt a masculine standpoint (Irigaray, 1985a; Lloyd, 1984; Seigfried, 1984; 1985).

Yet, Beauvoir herself was the beneficiary of a long history of women writers and activists who had challenged the derogatory stereotypes of women promoted by some men and who had argued for the education of women, in order to give them the same capacity to develop themselves as was accorded to men. Many women had criticised male domination in marriage and had offered alternative models of egalitarian friendship between the sexes that, arguably, led to a transformation of European culture and, in particular, the development of more egalitarian marriage relations (Green, 2021). As the cohort of female scholars grew, during the twentieth and twenty-first century, new research, often undertaken by women, made available a much richer selection of texts by past women than was available to Beauvoir. When she undertook her research in the Bibliothèque nationale, she would have been able to read a nineteenth-century collection of Christine de Pizan's poetry and Suzanne Solente's recent edition of her history of Charles V of France (Pizan, 1886; 1936–40). She might have come across extracts of other works by Pizan in Louise Keralio-Robert's multi-volume collection of the best works written in French by women, though I have not found mention of this work or its author in her publications (Keralio-Robert, 1786–9). But she would not have known any modern or even old French edition of Christine's most feminist work, *The Book of the City of Ladies*, which was not edited until 1975, when Maureen Cheney-Curnow undertook the task for a thesis at Vanderbilt University, in Tennessee. This book had never been printed in French, although an English translation had been published in 1521 (Curnow, 1975; Pizan, 1521). Since the publication of *The Second Sex*, the works of many of the women whom Beauvoir mentions in passing have become more widely available, works by other women have gained attention, and women's intellectual history has blossomed (Broad & Green, 2009; Green, 2014; Waithe, 1987–95). It no longer seems plausible to say that women have no history of their own, either in the sense of having written no history or in the sense of never having acted to make history. Nevertheless, there is no doubt that men have dominated past cultures and that any woman who wishes to participate in the production of the narrative through which her culture represents itself will have to engage with works written by men. Women may well figure in those works as the Other, but this does not imply that the women who engage with them lack their own independent subject status. In fact, often, they have been spurred to write as a result of the false, derogatory images of women confected by men. Yet the proposition that Beauvoir developed clearly spoke to women of her time, and it enabled her to develop an original account of the history of Western ideas, elements of which have since been taken up and developed, both by subsequent scholars and in popular culture.

Beauvoir's aim, in the first chapters of her work, is guided by the existentialist assumption that human culture and values are not determined by exterior conditions, despite the fact that material realities cannot be denied. She first considers biology, concluding that sexual difference is a reality, that their biology is 'an essential element of women's situation', and that the differences between male and female bodies implies that their hold on the world differs. Nevertheless, biology does not imply any fixed destiny, nor does it explain, according to what she says at this point, how woman has been subjugated or why she is the Other (*DS*, I.1.i, 78–9; *SSp*, 60; *SSbm*, 44–5). Similarly, with psychoanalysis, though it can provide an account of how the differences between male and female sexual anatomy – the possession or lack of the penis – can result in differences in the male and female subjective experience of the self, it cannot explain why women become the Other. Nor can the Marxist perspective, developed by Engels in *The Origin of the Family, Private Property and the State* (1884), which places the development of tools and consequent rise of private property at the heart of female subjection, really account for women's status as the Other. Beauvoir concludes that the phallus, the tool, and biological strength cannot by themselves explain women's status, arguing that they must be integrated into the overall perspective of human existence, 'the fundamental project of the existent transcending itself towards being' (*DS*, I.1.iii, 107–8; *SSp*, 86; *SSbm*, 69). This she sets out to do in her chapters on history.

In these chapters, she follows the thread offered by Hegel in order to develop an original account of the unfolding of history, which might be called a dialectic of sex. She does not use this term, which was coined twenty-one years later by Shulamith Firestone (Firestone, 1970). Rejecting the nineteenth-century pro-posal that there had been an ancient matriarchy, which had been used by Engels to claim that, with the rise of private property, there had been a historical defeat of women, Beauvoir asserts that the 'world has always belonged to males' (*DS*, I.2.i, 111; *SSp*, 87; *SSbm*, 73). She then offers her 'key to the whole mystery', an adaptation of Hegel's dialectic that 'explains' how it is that men develop an independent consciousness. This happens because it is in risking life that men come to recognise that life is not the highest value but is something that can serve greater ends (*DS*, I.2.i, 115; *SSp*, 89; *SSbm*, 76). Woman, she postulates, is biologically destined to repeat life, while at the same time she recognises that life has no value in itself, apart from these higher ends to which men aspire. These ends, which are recognised in the conscious sacrifice of life, are not concretely hers, since she 'is originally an existent who gives life and does not risk her life; there has never been a combat between the male and her'. Thus, Beauvoir concludes that Hegel's definition of the dependent consciousness, 'whose essential nature is simply to live or to be for another', applies particularly well to women (*DS*, I.2.i, 116; *SSp*, 90–1; *SSbm*, 76–7). This is not to say that women are completely unconscious – they do wish to transcend the present towards an open future – but Beauvoir asserts that it is men who concretely attain these values. This results in a situation that Beauvoir suggests is different from slavery. Rather, in transcending life and affirming spirit, men open up the future towards which women also aspire. Yet, paradoxically, the values that she vicariously adopts imply the subjection of nature and of woman.

One might question whether this is in fact an accurate representation of the values of all cultures. Many ancient societies appear to have valued nature, to have seen themselves as belonging to the land, or to have worshipped natural fecundity in various forms of goddess or great mother. But Beauvoir follows Lévi-Strauss in denying that these facts demonstrate that women ever wielded political power, repeating his assertion that 'authority, whether public or merely social, always belongs to men' (*DS*, I.2.ii, 124; *SSp*, 96; *SSbm*, 82). Women are goods that men possess, that are exchanged among men, so they are a kind of Absolute Other, and 'inessential', not other subjects with whom reciprocal relations can be set up. Even when nature and her goddesses are worshipped, it is men who set them up as idols. When he posits her as the essential, he is the one who is actually the essential. He is consciously creating values, which he can and will voluntarily overthrow as his early sense of his dependence in the face of unpredictable nature transforms, with the development of instruments and agriculture, into a sense of his capacity to dominate and control nature (*DS*, I.2.ii, 127; *SSp*, 98–9; *SSbm*, 84–5). In Beauvoir's hands, then, the rejected historical overthrow of women becomes a development in the values that men have created, which, at an early stage, involved their sense of dependence on powerful maternal, natural forces and later their overcoming of these forces; 'man frees himself definitively from subjugation by women' and women become no more than servants, initiating legends that capture men's representation of their triumph over nature in which 'the forces of order and light win over feminine chaos' (*DS*, I.2.ii, 135; *SSp*,103–4; *SSbm*, 90–1).

Although Beauvoir had denied that biology is destiny, there is a sense in which her transformed Hegelianism relies on biological difference to explain the purported fact that women have always been the Other of men and have never set themselves up as possessing a countervailing subjectivity. Men are hunters and warriors, women repeaters of mere species life. Indeed, despite the lip service that she gives to the existentialist account of metaphysical freedom, she also claims that 'the deep reason which from the beginning of history condemned woman to domestic work and prevented her from taking part in the construction of the world, is her subjection to the generative function' (*DS*, I.2.v, 203; *SSp*, 139; *SSbm*, 138). One reaction to this analysis was that offered by Firestone: that women's liberation would only happen with the transcendence of their biology (Firestone, 1970). But Firestone's prescriptions were fanciful, and it is questionable whether either women or men could deny the reality of sexual difference without falling into bad faith. In fact, Beauvoir seems to be reading back into prehistory features of women's situation that only arose after the establishment of herding and enclosed agriculture. Contemporary research into precolonial Australian societies, for instance, show that women's activities – gathering and cultivating roots and grains in their natural environmental ranges, hunting small animals, and fishing (including collecting shellfish, crustaceans, and eels, often through the use of traps, nets, and weirs) – produced the bulk of the society's food. There was no demos for women to be confined to, and the construction of their social world was exercised as much in their production of cloaks, baskets, nets, body art, other forms of artefact, and ceremonial and daily ornamentation as in men's participation in ceremony, tool making, and hunting. If there is an element of truth in the claim that men have always wielded authority, it resides in the facts that political power has been upheld by force, that it is men who have banded together to engage in warfare with other groups of men, and that it is men who most often use physical strength to enforce the law and dominate weaker elements within society. This feature of human societies can possibly be explained on the basis of biology, but does this justify the complete discounting of female cultural activity and authority that Beauvoir, following Lévi-Strauss, postulates?

In the introduction to her discussion of myths, Beauvoir adds a new element to the transformed Hegelian schematism that she had developed. She returns to the passage from *Phenomenology of Spirit* in which Hegel claims that 'being *for itself* ... comes forward in antithesis to the universal substance ... [and] preserves itself by separating itself from this inorganic nature, and by consuming it', noting that this process does not supply consciousness with a stable sense of itself, for in consuming the object it desires, consciousness destroys it (Hegel, 1977, §171, 107). This throws it back into its solipsistic immanence (*DS*, I.3.i, 239; *SSp*, 159; *SSbm*, 163). Beauvoir then takes from Hegel the idea that consciousness only recognises itself by differentiating itself from something that it is not – it requires another consciousness, which it recognises as consciousness, but which is not identical to it, to reflect it. 'It is the existence of other men which wrests each man from his immanence and allows him to achieve the truth of his being, to fulfil himself as transcendence, as escape towards an end, as project' (*DS*, I.3.i, 239–40; *SSp*, 159; *SSbm*, 163). But this results in the conflict between consciousnesses, in which each attempts to enslave or objectify the other. Although the resulting unhappy conflict between conscious selves could be overcome by a conversion of the kind she had discussed in *The Ethics of Ambiguity*, where each would posit both the other and itself as equally consciousness and object, such authenticity is difficult to achieve. Instead, she postulates, men find in women another consciousness that does not demand reciprocal recognition. Intermediary between unresponsive nature and an equal who would demand recognition, she allows him to escape the dialectic of master and slave (*DS*, I.3.i, 241; *SSp*, 172; *SSbm*, 164). She is an object of desire that can be consumed without thereby disappearing. Thus, she appears to be an Absolute Other who never demands reciprocity. Although she is like the slave in so far as she is the dependent consciousness, she is not like Hegel's slave, for she has never entered into conflict with men, and this gives her relationship with men a special character.

The exact relationship to Hegel's dialectic of Beauvoir's postulated non-dialectical recognition, which men thus attain with women, has perplexed Beauvoir's interpreters (Bauer, 2001; Bergoffen, 2017; Lundgren-Gothlin, 1996; Mussett, 2006). It stands out as a distinctive adaptation of both Hegel's original progress towards the reciprocal recognition of consciousnesses in Absolute Spirit and of the truncated dialectic of objectifying and being objectified that one finds in *Being and Nothingness*. Beauvoir's description of the attitude that men adopt towards women nevertheless contains definite echoes of the attitude of desire, as described by Sartre; woman is a consciousness that it seems possible to possess in her flesh (*DS*, I.3.i, 241; *SSp*, 160; *SSbm*, 164; Sartre, 1943, III.3.§2, 428–34; 1993, 388–94). In woman, man 'hopes to realise himself as a thing by possessing another being in its flesh, while at the same time being confirmed in his freedom by a docile freedom' (*DS*, I.3.i, 242; *SSp*, 161; *SSbm*, 165). This idea allows Beauvoir to offer a powerful ontological characterisation of the mythic identification of woman with nature. 'Appearing as the Other, woman, as a result, appears to exist in opposition to the nothingness that he recognises in himself, as a plenitude of being' (*DS*, I.3.i, 242; *SSp*, 161; *SSbm*, 165). Woman is identified with Nature, to which man stands in an ambivalent relationship: he exploits it as an exterior object and it crushes him, being beyond his capacity to control. 'It is a material envelope in which the soul is held prisoner', a metaphor that Luce Irigaray will develop at great length (*DS*, I.3.i, 245; *SSp*, 163; *SSbm*, 167; Irigaray, 1985a). Over many pages, Beauvoir develops the theme of the mythic female character of nature, of man's fear of reproduction and death, which he opposes with the equally mythic representation of his own transcendence of feminine chaos, finitude, fecundity, and death, towards rational order, infinity, immaterial spirit, and eternal life, images that will also be taken up and developed in a different key by Irigaray, Susan Bordo, Genevieve Lloyd, and other writers (Bordo, 1987; Irigaray, 1993; Lloyd, 1984).

This powerful characterisation of what is, for Beauvoir, a mythic structure adopted by men in order to flee the difficulty of reciprocal relations with others who are, like them, ambiguously subject and object – transcendence striving towards infinitude combined with finite materiality – has reappeared in various guises in subsequent feminist philosophies. In some it retains, to an extent, its mythic character, as it does in Genevieve Lloyd's *The Man of Reason*, in which it is put to work to account for the difficulty that women have in locating themselves within the philosophical tradition (Lloyd, 1984). Although only an effaced metaphor, the image of mind, reason, or consciousness, which men have posited as distinct from the engulfing feminine body, operates so as to constitute the substance of philosophy (Lloyd, 1986). In other writers, male transcendence is used to characterise the philosophical tradition as a continuation of the mythic oppositions described by Beauvoir (Bordo, 1987). In others it becomes a truth about what it is to be male or female, resulting, by the 1980s, in the emergence of ecofeminist philosophies in which the identification of woman with nature is used to ally women's liberation with that of nature (Gray, 1981; Merchant, 1981; Plumwood, 1989; Salleh, 1992; Warren, 1990). The earliest example of this ecofeminist tendency came from Françoise Eaubonne and was continued in Irigaray's later work (Eaubonne, 1974; Irigaray, 1989). In many cases it is combined with elements from psychoanalysis and tends towards essentialist theories of masculine and feminine difference, which are quite at odds with Beauvoir's avowed existentialism. Indeed, paradoxically, although she was later criticised as a philosopher of equality who desired to efface sexual difference, her account of what she represents as a masculine mythology, adopted in the service of men's bad faith, provided later authors with ample material to be drafted into the service of subsequent feminisms of difference (Gross, 1990; Irigaray, 1991; 1993). Mythic structures were thus problematically transformed into psychic and even essential realities (*TCF*, 508; *ASD*, 458; Green, 1994).

There is no doubt that the Western tradition has tended to imagine nature as feminine, but had Beauvoir taken more time to explore women's philosophical imaginary, she would have discovered rather different metaphoric adaptations of this identification. Historical women have had no difficulty in imagining nature as an intelligent, female agent. Margaret Cavendish, for instance, says, 'though Nature is old, yet she is not a Witch, but a grave, wise, methodical Matron, ordering her Infinite family, which are her several parts, with ease and facility' (Cavendish, 1664, 302). She wittily deconstructs Descartes' dualism, denying that nature needs 'a Spiritual Nurse, to teach her to go, or to move' (Broad et al., 2006; Cavendish, 1664, 149–50). Nature, or matter, is, she believes, itself infinite and self-moving. Equally, philosophy, wisdom, and transcendent reason can take on a mythic, feminine persona, as they do in Christine de Pizan's *Book of the City of Ladies*, in her *Advision Cristine*, and in Boethius's *Consolation of Philosophy*, which partly inspired her (Boethius, 1999; Broad & Green, 2006; Pizan, 1983; 2001). For Mary Wollstonecraft as well, with the advent of the French Revolution, reason becomes a woman who has 'at last, shown her captivating face, beaming with benevolence' (Wollstonecraft, 1989, 22). Beauvoir overdetermines the mythic characterisation of woman as nature, a bodily other that offers up its yielding recognition to a masculine transcendence, by ignoring, or being unaware of, an underappreciated tradition of countervailing myth, often promoted by women.

The first volume of *The Second Sex* thus develops an original philosophical schematism, inspired by Hegel's *Phenomenology of Spirit*, in order to account for the supposed fact that woman has always been the Other of man without opposing to him her own independent consciousness. The second volume has a somewhat different character, setting out to capture the lived experience of being a woman. It offers a sociological account of women's situations in the West, dependent on available early twentieth-century descriptions of women's experiences, coloured by Beauvoir's own personal background. The existentialist schema of the first volume is less apparent but re-emerges in the descriptions of women's attitudes towards themselves and others, particularly in its later sections on women's 'justifications'.

The second volume begins with the famous line, 'one is not born a woman: but becomes one' (*DS*, II.1.i, 13; *SSp*, 273; *SSbm*, 294).[5] Although Beauvoir then repeats her claim that women are not destined by biology, psychology, or economics to become what they are socially, and although she had prefaced the volume with a phrase attributed to Sartre, 'part victims, part accomplices, like everyone', it has been easy for her readers to interpret this opening line as implying that women are socially determined to play a role not of their own making. Indeed, much of the power of her work lies in the descriptions of the social pressures that mould feminine behaviour, and women's subjective responses to those pressures, which result in a reading according to which the sentence expresses a belief in the social construction of gender roles (Offen,

---

[5] For controversy over how this should be translated, see (Mann and Ferrari, 2017).

2017, 11). The existentialist concept of 'choosing to become', or of making oneself be, emphasised by Julia Kristeva and Jennifer McWeeny, is often obscured by the lengthy descriptions of the forces that propel women to adopt traditional, feminine characteristics, which, Beauvoir contended, showed that the dissimilarities between the sexes are 'of a cultural not a natural order' (*FCh*, I.259; *FC*, 196; Kristeva, 2018, 352–3; McWeeny, 2017).

It is in adolescence that these pressures begin to weigh heavily. Despite all the difficulties of childhood, Beauvoir suggests that, as children, girls experience their autonomy and transcendence. Adolescence is a time of transition during which they await their fate: Man. Menstruation makes matters worse, being represented by Beauvoir as a painful state of oppression and alienation from the body. She observes that during adolescence girls give up active sports, become timid, and lose ground in intellectual and artistic fields (*DS*, II.1.ii, 88–96; *SSp*, 327–32; *SSbm*, 352–7). The demands of modesty limit their freedom and they begin to experience themselves as objects of an exterior gaze, being encouraged to turn towards a self-conscious narcissism. Although some of Beauvoir's descriptions relate more to the situation of young women in mid-twentieth-century Europe than to that of the much freer and more highly sexualised culture of the developed world in the early twenty-first century, her Hegel-inspired existentialist account of relations with others offers a powerful analysis of the ambiguities in the behaviour of young women that continue to resonate. There is a conflict between a girl's narcissism and the revolt that she feels in being captured by the male gaze and reduced to mere fleshy immanence. While she makes an object of herself, it is one that is an idol, in which she recognises herself, and that allows her to bask in male attention, but as soon as she is objectified, she feels shame. 'So long as she feels responsible for her charm, which she seems to exercise freely, she is enchanted by her victories: but in so far as her features, her figure, her flesh are givens to which she submits, she wants to deny possession of them to this foreign, indiscreet freedom that desires them' (*DS*, II.1.ii, 118–19; *SSp*, 347–8; *SSbm*, 375). As a subject she wishes to dominate the other, enslaving him through her desirability, but once he reaches out to possess her, she herself becomes no more than an object of desire. At this juncture, the metaphysical framework of the conflict between consciousnesses throws considerable light on behaviours that can appear to men to be no more than hypocritical teasing. At others, the schema through which Beauvoir analyses woman's situation results in a somewhat distorted account, or at least one that overlooks perspectives that don't fit in with her metaphysical assumptions.

The chapter on sexual initiation is particularly bleak, emphasising man's active initiation of the sex act. 'Since she is object her inertia does not profoundly alter her natural role . . . one can even go to bed with a dead woman' (*DS*, II.1.iii, 148; *SSp*, 368; *SSbm*, 396). Steeped in nineteenth-century traditions of feminine sexual modesty, horror at the thought of penetration, and assumptions about girls' sexual ignorance, Beauvoir accepts that, 'however deferential and courteous a man might be, the first penetration is always a violation' (*DS*, II.1.iii, 161; *SSp*, 376; *SSbm*, 406). She quotes extensively from William Stekel's, *Frigidity in Women*, reinforcing the impression that women fear sex and seldom achieve satisfaction (Stekel, 1943). She concludes that,

> Even if she adapts herself more or less completely to her passive role, woman remains frustrated as an active individual. She does not envy him his organ of possession, but his prey. It is a curious paradox that man lives in a sensual world of sweetness, softness and tenderness, a feminine world, whereas woman silences herself in the male world which is hard and severe.
> (*DS*, II.1.iii, 188–9; *SSp*, 394; *SSbm*, 427–8)

Women, she goes on to say, dream of possessing a soft, smooth, feminine lover, explaining the wide appeal of lesbianism – then considered to be a sinful aberration – for women, expressing her own, concealed, experience of lesbian love (Kirkpatrick, 2019, 137–86). In the following chapter, she openly discusses, without judgement, the many different forms of feminine homosexuality, as well as what would now be called cases of intersex and transgender individuals, undoubtedly contributing to the early movement to normalise what were, at the time, generally characterised as deviant forms of sexuality.

In later interviews, Beauvoir expresses some regret in relation to the way in which female eroticism was treated in these chapters and confessed that her views had since changed considerably (Bainbrigge, 1995, 160; Schwarzer, 1984). Paradoxically, one could claim that it is through them that the language that she introduced, according to which woman is the Other of man, has had the greatest impact on the development of popular culture and late twentieth-century feminism, for the idea that women are sex objects, and that it is objectification by an alien male sexual rapaciousness that is at the heart of women's oppression, has become ubiquitous. Although she does not use the phrase 'sexual objectification', she is now read as claiming that it is responsible for women's oppression (Kirkpatrick, 2019, 262). An implicit solution, that women can only achieve an authentic eroticism through lesbianism, has been widely adopted (Dworkin, 1981; Jeffreys, 1990; MacKinnon, 1987; Rich, 1980). Although these authors do not in general acknowledge their debt to Beauvoir, the powerful movement against sexual objectification and pornography that has arisen since the 1980s develops images similar to those found in her account of sexual initiation, divorcing them from the metaphysical and existentialist under-pinning of her essay. Beauvoir saw herself as describing a social situation in which women's sexual agency had been closed off to her, but she believed, at least in principle, that sexual agency was something that women could regain. Near the end of the book, she admits the existence of many sexually egalitarian couples for whom 'notions of victory and defeat are replaced by the idea of exchange' (*DS*, II.4. Conclusion, 648; *SSp*, 683; *SSbm*, 779). She believed that, although male sovereignty had been ubiquitous, it also con-stituted a kind of bad faith, an attempt, through the possession of the flesh of women in which consciousness resides, to experience their transcendence without facing up to the difficulties of mutual recognition. She is vague as to how the social situation will come about in which mutual recognition between the sexes is achieved, yet she is committed to the possibility of an eroticism in which each lives the ambiguity of their condition. For,

> Man is like woman flesh, hence passive, plaything of his hormones and of the species; and she is like him, in the midst of her carnal consenting fever, voluntary gift, activity; each lives in their own way the strange equivocation of [conscious] being made body. (*DS*, II.4. Conclusion, 648; *SSp*, 683; *SSbm*, 779)

But the later theory of sexual objectification offers no positive representation of heterosexuality. Cut off from its original metaphysical underpinnings, the description of male sexuality as domination becomes implicitly essentialist, and although writers such as Catharine MacKinnon claim that eroticism and gender are socially constructed, the absence in their writing of any positive representation of heterosexuality is the natural correlate of the assumption that any form of sexual objectification by men of women constitutes, in itself, sexual oppression.

Beauvoir seems to have assumed that she could eclectically combine Lévi-Strauss's structuralist anthropology, Engels's Marxist account of the role of the family and private property, and existentialism to develop an account of women's situation. But fundamental elements of these outlooks are incompat-ible with her existentialism. Even though she rejected the sufficiency of Engels's account of the origin of women's subordination in the rise of private property, she represents her book as owing 'much to Marxism', and she often implies that women are less oppressed in societies where ownership is collect-ive (*FCh*, I.265; *FC*, 200). Thus, Sparta is assumed to have accorded women greater agency than did Athens, and women's liberation requires an 'economic evolution' (*DS*, I.2.iii, 147, II.2.x, 515; *SSp*, 112, 595; *SSbm*, 99, 680). But, as she had noted earlier, Marxism, in general, is incompatible with the existential-ist emphasis on individual liberty, and, apart from extreme cases of slavery, it remains unclear how different economic systems impact differentially on meta-physical freedom. Even more obvious than the tension between existentialism and Marxism is its conflict with the structuralist orientation of Lévi-Strauss's anthropology.[6] According to structuralism, human conscious decisions are determined by the social and linguistic structures of the society within which individuals operate. Human freedom is a myth. Early on, Beauvoir had been impressed by the Bergsonian idea that there is a phenomenal reality, available to the senses, that cannot be fully captured in the sharp but inadequate contours of public language. The structuralists posit, rather, that there is no unmediated phenomenal experience. What we see and feel is determined by the linguistic structures that we inherit from our community. This combines rather neatly with the Marxist concept of ideology, according to which beliefs are determined by underlying economic relations, being ways of representing reality that are in the interests of the dominant class. Linguistic structures become the intermediaries by means of which power relations colonise minds and form compliant subjects. Even as she was publishing *The Second Sex*, the phenomenological and exist-entialist outlook that Beauvoir shared with Sartre was being overshadowed by the rise of structuralism, so that her representation of women as objects of male desire came to be read through this lens. Later, pornography emerged as the sexual sign system par excellence and the vehicle by means of which gender is socially constructed (Dworkin, 1981; 1987; MacKinnon, 1987). Beauvoir's critique of objectifying forms of male sexuality, which she interpreted as instances of bad faith and an attempt to escape the difficulty of reciprocal relations, was replaced by the claim that the language of heterosexual pornog-raphy creates the reality of male sexual desire. The contrast between her outlook and that of the later anti-pornographers is clear in their quite different attitudes to the Marquis de Sade, yet there is a clear sense in which the anti-pornographers build on her claim that woman is the Other of man (*MBS*; Butler, 2003; Green, 2000).

In the light of the impact of Marxism on her thought, Beauvoir's account of the way women are represented can be interpreted as detailing patriarchal ideology, but her descriptions then inherit a general problem faced by all appeals to ideology, which is that, in order for beliefs to be ideological, there must be some true perspective. It is insufficient to say that the perspective of the oppressed is true, since the oppressed do not always agree with each other, nor is

---

[6] Sartre attempted to resolve these conflicts in his *Critique of Dialectical Reason* but failed to convince Lévi-Strauss of the success of his project, and the general consensus, articulated, for instance, by Foucault, has been that the triumph of structuralism was the death knell of the theory of the free, conscious subject nostalgically presumed to exist by Sartre (Doran, 2013; Eribon, 1993; Lévi-Strauss, 1966; Sartre, 1976).

there always agreement as to who are the oppressed. The outlook of white, Western women, such as Beauvoir, has been criticised from the perspective of black people and indigenous people (Gines, 2010). Beauvoir herself has been accused of writing from a misogynist perspective, apparent when she says of some women that, 'their vain arrogance, their radical incapability, their stubborn ignorance, turn them into the most useless beings, the most idiotic that the human species has ever produced', a sharp invective that she directed at upperclass women (*DS*, II.2.x, 515; *SSp*, 594; *SSbm*, 679). This is a judgement that, given her own class background, might well be judged to be a spectacular expression of bad faith (or self-loathing). Not only has her assumption, that the pursuit of transcendence is of value, been deemed incompatible with a womancentred philosophy, but such passages express a general disdain for women's concerns and lives. In particular, her accounts of motherhood and marriage show considerable contempt for the attitudes, concerns, and projects of many ordinary women. This was a particular focus of attack when her book first appeared, for she represents motherhood as rarely an authentic choice, summing it up as a 'strange compromise of narcissism, altruism, dream, sincerity, bad faith, devotion and cynicism' (*FCh*, I.266; *FC*, 201; *DS*, II.2.vi; *SSp*, 492; *SSbm*, 570). Long before the movement to legalise abortion, Beauvoir had begun her chapter on motherhood with a call for birth control and the legalisation of abortion, in order to change the prevalence of unplanned pregnancy. She quotes Stekel, 'Prohibition of abortion is an immoral law, since it must forcibly be broken every day, every hour' (*DS*, II.2.vi, 338–9; *SSbm*, 546).[7] Not surprisingly, this caused outrage in some quarters. In general, the very ambivalent attitude that Beauvoir evinced towards pregnancy and motherhood shocked conservative sensibilities in a still largely Catholic country.

Given the opposition between transcendence and immanence that structures her ontology, it is unsurprising that she presents pregnancy as a threat. It is the engulfment of consciousness by the flesh, 'the opposition between subject and object disappears; she and the child who swells in her form an ambivalent couple that life submerges; snared by nature she is plant and animal, a collection of colloids, an incubator, an egg' (*DS*, II.2.vi, 345; *SSp*, 477; *SSbm*, 552). Woman has become the passive instrument of the reproduction of life. Of women who enjoy pregnancy and have many children, Beauvoir says that they are not mothers, but 'breeders' who 'eagerly seek the possibility of alienating their liberty to the benefit of their flesh'. As flesh, being pure inertia, cannot embody even a degraded transcendence, such a woman is trapped in the

---

[7] This sentence was not translated by Parshley, presumably because it was deemed too inflammatory.

'great cycle of the species' (*DS*, II.2.vi, 346–7; *SSp*, 478–9; *SSbm*, 552–3). It is certainly true that, in pregnancy, a woman becomes particularly aware of bodily processes largely beyond her control. Yet one cannot help thinking that, in these passages, Beauvoir becomes enmeshed in the masculine mythology that she had detailed so extensively in the first volume of her work. In Plato's *Symposium*, Diotima, Socrates' philosophical midwife, represents sexual desire, pregnancy, and birth as a corporeal bringing-forth of beauty, a repetition of species life directed towards infinity, that is inferior to the spiritual engendering of laws, through which men reproduce culture. In her refusal to see pregnancy and motherhood as valuable projects that can, and often do, involve women's transcendence of the past towards an imagined future, Beauvoir likewise accepts that the artisan, or man of action, achieves a level of transcendence unavailable to women. Yet what justifies this, other than men's past denigration? The marathon runner, the body builder, the competitive swimmer could equally be said to 'alienate their liberty to the benefit of their flesh' as, in the effort of their physical exertion, their consciousness becomes subsumed by its bodily effects. Yet we understand this state as a temporary situation, submitted to in the pursuit of higher goals and compatible with the achievement of other ends. Why not take the same attitude to pregnancy? Beauvoir's own situation seems to have encouraged the assumption that motherhood and transcendence inevitably conflict.

Beauvoir had assumed, in her own life, that being a writer and being a mother were incompatible, claiming that, as a result of wanting to write, she had never wanted to have children (Patterson, 1989, 296; *FA*, 91; *PL*, 78). To assume that this must be the case is to perpetuate elements of the past situation of women that have made it difficult for them to achieve historical recognition. It is to overlook that one of differences between men's and women's situations is that, in the past, men have been able to pursue artistic careers as well as founding families, while women only have the same freedom when motherhood does not present itself as an insurmountable barrier to literary or other success. Sartre and Beauvoir attempted to subvert the usual implications of childlessness by adopting younger women, who would commit themselves to perpetuating their legacy, yet this can hardly become a universal strategy. Assuming the incompatibility of motherhood and active self-expression thus seems to be succumbing to a form of the old 'biology is destiny' myth. It is true, as some have pointed out, that Beauvoir does not deny the possibility of an authentic motherhood, which she imagines as possible in a situation where 'the society would assume charge of the children', thus making motherhood compatible with a career (*DS*, II.4, Conclusion, 644; *SSp*, 680–1; *SSbm*, 776–7). Yet this solution glosses over the fact that, if motherhood and childcare are not projects compatible with transcendence, the lives of an underclass of mothers and child-carers will be sacrificed to the care of the children of elite women, a situation that has tended to develop in wealthy communities, where women with careers often depend on poor, black, or immigrant women to look after their children and to take on other domestic tasks. One needs a more positive conception of motherhood, as constituting an important form of participation in society, compatible with other forms of construction of culture, in order for women to have the same ability to develop themselves as do men. This form of criticism of Beauvoir's outlook began to be developed during the 1980s, though the tensions between mothering and autonomy remain significant (O'Brien, 1981; Ruddick, 1990).

Beauvoir's ambivalent and somewhat hostile attitude towards motherhood was arguably also coloured by her own relationship with her mother. In an interview, she claimed that mother–daughter relationships are generally cata-strophic, and her relationship with her own mother was often strained (Schwarzer, 1984, 91). This is symptomatic of an underlying difficulty in the whole method of attempting to combine a metaphysical outlook with concrete description that is pursued by Beauvoir in *The Second Sex*, as well as in her fiction. Elsewhere, in a passage where she asserts that she did not regard herself as a philosopher, she rejects the 'lunacy known as a "philosophical system" from which those who have constructed them, derive that obsessional attitude which endows their tentative patterns with universal insight and applicability' (*FA*, 254; *PL*, 221). Applying this critique, she herself claims that, in the face of class, race, and individual difference, it is as absurd to speak of 'woman' in general as to imagine 'eternal man' (*DS*, II.2.x, 515; *SSp*, 638; *SSbm*, 679). Yet the method she adopts encourages just this tendency. Descriptions of concrete individual experience, when interpreted in the light of a metaphysical schema-tism, are in danger of being universalised and generalised beyond the specific temporal and cultural moment of the experienced reality. This is evident both in Beauvoir's account of motherhood and in the related reading of the woman in love, which universalises features of Beauvoir's own experience and sentiments along with those of women of her class, culture, and time.

Beauvoir's description of the woman in love is wedged between that of the narcissist and the mystic, as one of women's justifications, attitudes that Beauvoir describes as strategies that individual women adopt in order to attempt to justify their existence within their immanence. These are projects converting 'servitude into sovereign freedom', or one might say in different language, in which individuals freely choose to adopt attitudes of subjection and objectifica-tion (*DS*, II.2.x, 516; *SSp*, 639; *SSbm*, 680). Narcissism is a peculiar version of this tendency, for the narcissist is both the transcendent subject who loves herself and the object of that love. The woman in love also objectifies herself but does so through the agency of a lover. She tries to 'overcome her situation as inessential object by assuming it', and, since men present themselves as sovereign subjects, with whom equality is not permitted, she makes a religion of love and posits her lover as a divinity, the supreme reality to which she devotes herself, through whose transcendence she vicariously realises her being (*DS*, II.3.xii; *SSp*, 656; *SSbm*, 700). The woman in love is like the mystic, who annihilates herself before God, but the former makes man into a God, while the latter makes herself God's bride and lover.

The woman in love, who attempts to live through her lover and is destroyed, or at the very least deeply threatened and disappointed in life, by the threat or reality of her lover leaving her, is a recurrent figure in Beauvoir's novels. Françoise, in *She Came to Stay*; Régine, in *All Men are Mortal*; Dominque, in *Les Belles Images*; and Paula, in *The Mandarins* are all women whose lives and sense of self-worth depend on the love of a man who does not have the same need for them. There are echoes in these relationships of Beauvoir's youthful infatuation with Jacques, and the dependence on the love of another that she attempted to keep at bay in her relationship with Sartre. Dependent love was a temptation that she had felt, but one that she consciously and proudly resisted (*PL*, 80). In *The Second Sex*, Beauvoir represents the woman in love as wanting to serve her lover and being justified by the existence into which she is integrated (*DS*, II.3.xii, 550; *SSp*, 660; *SSbm*, 707). The lover wants to be identified with her beloved and her supreme happiness consists in being part of a 'we' in which she is recognised by him. But the dependence of the woman becomes a burden for the man and equally harbours the danger of disillusionment for the woman when the man to whom she has devoted herself fails to live up to her high ideals. In these descriptions, Beauvoir has captured the situation of many women of her time and place, but it is arguable that she has overextended the common situation of twentieth-century, middle-class women, who had little option but to live vicariously through the achievements of the men they had loved and married, with the situation of women at all times and places.

In opposition to the idolatrous but dependent love that women offer to men, through whom they wish to justify their existence, Beauvoir offers the alternative of an 'authentic love' that would 'take on the other's contingence, that is his lacks, limitations and originary gratuitousness'. Such a love would be no salvation but an 'interhuman relation' and 'the reciprocal relation of two freedoms' (*DS*, II.3.xii, 554, 571; *SSp*, 619, 631; *SSbm*, 711, 723). In her autobiographical memoirs, beginning with *Memoirs d'une jeaune fille rangée*, published in the late fifties, when she herself had reached her fiftieth year, Beauvoir wrote an account of her own life as one attempt to live out such an 'authentic love' (*MJ*; *MD*). In these autobiographies, she found a more natural medium through which to capture the concrete realities of lived experience from a distinctive ontological perspective than that of the novel. Whereas, in her novels, the metaphysical framework within which she structures her character's lives can become forced, in her memoirs, her own development as a writer and thinker provides a natural starting point for a meditation on existence, the unfolding of time, relations with others, and the possibility of an authentic and fulfilled life. If *The Second Sex* plays the role in Beauvoir's oeuvre that she attributes to *Being and Nothingness* in Sartre's, of being an account of humanity in bad faith, her memoirs attempt to offer an alternative positive image of a woman striving to live according to her own conception of honesty and freedom. Yet sometimes the autobiographies gloss over uncomfortable facts. Recently, Kate Kirkpatrick has used previously unavailable material to question the extent to which earlier biographers had too uncritically swallowed Beauvoir's narrative (Kirkpatrick, 2019; see also Bair, 1990; Rowley, 2005). Pointing to the lacunae in the account of her bisexual affairs and the extent to which both she and Sartre were less than honest with their friends and lovers, she questions whether Beauvoir lived up to the ideal of authenticity to which she aspired. Yet, whatever her actual bad faith, the biographies allowed her to reflect on the inadequacies of certain metaphysical assumptions and to introduce philosophical themes into a novelistic narrative in a perfectly natural way. Without the continuing reflection on her life offered in her autobiographies, Beauvoir would not have achieved either the notoriety or breadth of audience that she did. They extend the last chapter of *The Second Sex*, that on 'the independent woman', over the course of a lifetime, offering a model, albeit a problematic one, of her existence as a free, female subject who understood her fulfilment to lie in her transcendence of the concrete situation into which she had been born, towards a chosen future. But, along with her later essays, they attest to a change in her own political and philosophical orientation that conflicts with the humanistic existentialism of her middle years.

4 Autobiography and Politics

At the conclusion of the second instalment of her autobiography, *The Prime of Life*, Beauvoir represents the war as a watershed period in her life. As an adolescent she had felt stifled by the constraints of a well-ordered bourgeois life, and her activities were governed by the requirements of propriety and her mother's overbearing presence. Success at university had offered her freedom and economic independence, in which she had revelled. Despite her great love for Sartre, she declined the opportunity of marrying him, so that they could be posted together, and took up a teaching post at Marseille, where she learned to live independently, acquiring a passion for solitary rambles in the sparsely populated Provençal hinterland of this port. She was an individualist, determined to enjoy what life had to offer, imagining herself to be living the life of Katherine Mansfield's 'solitary woman' (*FA*, 118; *PL*, 85). The war was to change all this, bringing with it fear and scarcity, throwing her existence into uncertainty and turmoil, making it impossible to ignore the extent to which we are hostage to the actions of others for our freedom and happiness. It fractured the self-absorption and insouciance of her early adult life, forced the recognition of the possibility of death, caused the death of friends, and constituted a break with her earlier self, which gave her the critical distance from her past necessary to write a successful novel, as she had for a long time desired to do (*FA*, 684; *PL*, 606).

She Came to Stay, completed during the war, chronicled a world inhabited by individuals. *The Second Sex* began to consider how the individual is shaped by society. Subsequently, Beauvoir repudiated the individualism of her own former attitudes and fell more and more under the sway of Marxism. Yet one theme from her existentialist background would continue to haunt her works: Heidegger's being towards death (Heinämaa, 2010). Death, over which she had agonised as a child, was rehabilitated in *All Men Are Mortal* as the necessary precondition for finite human projects, the source of the value of life, and the 'common link between the individual and mankind', while also remaining the source of loneliness and separation (*THM*; *MM*; *FA*, 685; *PL*, 607; La Caze, 2004–5, 148). The very solipsism of her early years made death, the cessation of her own consciousness, appear impossible, the annihilation of the world, while the death of a friend, even more acutely than their living, thrust her out of her solipsism and into the recognition of the finite fragility of her own partial perspective. When she heard of the death of Camus, who had been a good friend, but with whom she and Sartre had fallen out politically, Beauvoir experienced the 'world through his dead eyes'. She 'had gone over to the other side where there is nothing', realising 'how everything still continued to exist' though she/he was no longer there (*FCh*, II.278; *FC*, 497). The death of the other thus wrenches her out of her solipsism, while plunging her into dismay at the realisation that, when she is gone, the world will continue without her. Her almost obsessive turn towards autobiographical writing attempts to cheat death, to capture on the page, in well-chosen words, the evanescent passage of her life, the lush warm grasses of Meyrignac, the damp smell of Parisian autumns, the sharp clear vistas of Provençal treks. Despite her early commitment to Bergson's claim that the multifaceted shimmer of our perceptual experience escapes the dry rigour of words, in later years she worked tirelessly to capture in words the unique thread of her experience, to crystalise it for futurity, and to break out from the separation of consciousnesses by means of that ubiquitous linguistic vehicle through which we share our experience with members of our linguistic and cultural community.

After the success of the Goncourt-prize-winning *Les Mandarins* (*LM*; *TM*), which gives a fictionalised account of the conflict among different elements of the left during and after the war, Beauvoir became famous. This period, during which the Algerians and Vietnamese began to throw off colonial French rule in viciously opposed movements of national liberation, saw her deepening her critique of capitalism and colonialism. The Algerian conflict moved her deeply. She was appalled by and ashamed of the French army's resort to torture, rape, and illegal killing in Algeria and, in a preface to Gisèle Halimi's *Djamila Boupacha*, published an impassioned account of the way in which these activities had been kept secret and the circumstances that led to the publication of the book (*PolW*, 272–82; Halimi, 1962). Two motifs, Marxism and being towards death, engendered two long essays, neither of which was nearly so successful or influential as *The Second Sex*. The first, *The Long March*, was the result of a visit to China in 1955 (*LoM*; *LoMe*). The second, *Old Age*, was prompted by Beauvoir's own confrontation with her ageing self (*LV*; *OA*). Like *The Second Sex*, these essays are compilations of the available historical, biological, sociological, and anthropological data concerning their subjects, but unlike it, they are not structured around the Hegelian conflict between consciousnesses that provided the framework for the earlier work (Deutscher, 2017, 440; Stoller, 2014, 2–3). Instead, a Marxist orientation often prevails. Beauvoir does not discuss at length the extent to which she continued to accept that her adaptation of the Hegelian conflict between consciousnesses was an accurate analysis of the origins of women's subordinate position, but the orientation of these later works to an extent undermines it. In *Force of Circumstance*, she endorses the account based on 'facts of supply and demand' that she had adopted in her book on China and indicates that, had she written *The Second Sex* later, she would not 'base the notion of woman as *other* and the Manichaean argument it entails' on 'an idealistic and *a priori* struggle of consciousnesses' (*FCh*, I.207; *FC*, 202). But to have done so would have robbed her work of all its originality, which essentially resides in the adaptation of Hegel's master/slave dialectic to account for the relationship between men and women.

Written during the Cold War, *The Long March* is both a travelogue and an apology for the communist government of China. It emphasises the extent to which order and cleanliness had been achieved in Chinese cities, which had, prior to the revolution, been renowned for their disease, poverty, opium addiction, and filth (*LoMe*, 52–3, 448–50). Beauvoir's turn towards Marxism is particularly evident in her discussion of the family. Whereas, in *The Second*

Sex, she had argued against the Marxist view that family structures are fully determined by economic realities and that the rise of private property had caused the subordination of women, in *The Long March* she offers an economic explanation of the long persistence, in China, of extended patriarchal families cohabiting under one roof.

This results, she claims, from China's late industrialisation. In Europe, the transition from the patriarchal to conjugal or companionate marriage is assumed to have coincided with the advent of industry, moveable property, and a working-class proletariat. The traditional Chinese family 'is to be explained by the country's agrarian economy' (*LoMe*, 127). Yet she also subscribes to the widely held view that women were more thoroughly oppressed within the traditional Chinese family than in almost any other country. She explains this by the fact that 'in every civilization the history of women's rights is directly linked to the history of inheritance which has evolved as a dependent variable of the changing economic and social complex' (*LoMe*, 130). This, she claims in a footnote, she had tried to show in *The Second Sex*. It was because inheritance in China was exclusively male that women were unable to achieve any kind of economic autonomy or other form of independence.

Yet, this kind of purely economic explanation of the differences in women's social situation in China and Europe is not particularly illuminating. From the twelfth to fifteenth centuries, both Europe and China were agrarian economies, the family was governed by a patriarch, and inheritance was generally male. However, in Europe, daughters could occasionally inherit, when a male heir was lacking, and, in many jurisdictions, widows could own property in their own right and operate with almost the same legal and financial autonomy as men. In China, lack of literary talent was considered a virtue in women, whereas in Europe it was not impossible for elite women, such as Hildegard von Bingen, Heloise, or Christine de Pizan, to achieve significant literary success. These differences are difficult to explain on purely economic grounds. Arguably, it was Christianity, with its emphasis on the virtue of chastity and valorisation of monogamy, that allowed some women to remain virgins and opened up the possibility for widows to resist remarriage and operate independently, if they wished. Furthermore, monogamy was more prone to result in a lack of a male heir than the polygamy practised in China and elsewhere, so that in Europe, female inheritance became a fairly widespread, though often contested, practice. In China, excess daughters were killed at birth; in Europe, they were consigned to a convent. It is such cultural factors, rather than pure economic circumstances, that are at least part of the explanation of the differences between the situation of women during periods of similar economic development in China and Europe. In Europe, the rise of conjugal marriage coincides with the emergence of Protestantism, so, since Marxists like to explain Protestantism as the result of an economic evolution, a committed Marxist is unlikely to be swayed by the foregoing observations. Yet reading the works of the women mentioned by Beauvoir in *The Second Sex* suggests that the transformation from patriarchal to conjugal or companionate marriage in Europe was as much the result of women's participation in the ferment of ideas, brought about by the rise of vernacular literature and the printing press, as by any significant change in economic production (Green, 2021). This is not the place to pursue the question of the origins of conjugal marriage, but by uncritically adopting a Marxist line, Beauvoir neglects the opportunity of more thoroughly exploring the reasons for the differences in the situation of women in pre-industrial Europe and in China.

Her discussion of old age is also largely framed by Marxist rhetoric, though Beauvoir here also returns to the way individuals are treated as other, in order to describe the situation of the aged. Following Marxist assumptions, it is, she says, 'the ruling class that imposes their status upon the old' (*LV*, 230; *OA*, 216). But this sheds no light on the difference in attitudes towards old age in different societies, it being something of a tautology to say that those with power impose various kinds of status on themselves and others. Her own earlier account of China indicates how tradition, philosophy, and culture impact the respect afforded the aged, whose status also remains tied to class and sex. In the patriarchal Chinese family, the old woman, once she is a successful mother who has produced grown sons, will govern her unmarried daughters and daughters-in-law, and be accorded considerable authority and respect within the multigenerational household. This is a status rarely achieved by the aged female in contemporary Western societies, where she is often consigned to an institution and the negligent care of strangers.

As with *The Second Sex*, which is most successful when it turns to giving an account of the experience of being a woman in the culture to which Beauvoir belonged, so with *Old Age*. The second volume of *The Second Sex* describes 'l'expérience vécu'; similarly, the fifth chapter of *Old Age* is subtitled, 'expérience vécu du corps' (*LV*, 301). It is when she turns to describing the phenomenon of ageing, as it is experienced by her and her contemporaries, that her account is most authentic. Disappointingly, however, the old woman features very rarely among the subjects whose experience of ageing she recounts. Her own experience had piqued her interest in the subject, yet, although she acknowledges in an appendix that there are many more very old women than very old men, the accounts that she exploits are largely those of men who, like her, have left a literary legacy. In the last pages of *Force of Circumstance*, she had already observed that the most significant thing that had happened to her was that she had grown old. The first story in the collection *The Woman Destroyed* also focuses on a couple struggling with this realisation (*FR*, 9–84; *WDes*, 9–85). Like that of the characters in this novel, the world around her had narrowed and ceased to be full of new wonders to explore. A time had come when she and Sartre no longer met up with startling new intellectual superiors who possessed the 'magical prestige' that even ordinary individuals can have in the eyes of a child (*FCh*, II.502; *FC*, 669). For years, she had thought of her work as stretching out before her, but by 1963 it already appeared to exist in the past. In *The Second Sex* she had attempted to characterise the situation of women; in *Old Age* she turns to considering the temporality of existence from the perspective of someone who is approaching the end of their life. Her mother's death was undoubtedly also a cause of this turn to a meditation on our mortality, for it had affected her far more deeply than she had expected, as she recounts in *A Very Easy Death* (*MTD*, 151–3; *VED*, 89–90). It brought with it a softening of her attitude towards her mother, evident in the last volume of her autobiography, as well as reinforcing her recognition that she was entering into a new phase, that of old age (*TCF*, Prologue; *ASD*, vii, Prologue).

The old person who, when young, had seen themselves as projecting their existence towards an open future, on which they had hoped to make an impact, is forced to face up to the finitude of their existence, and often looks back nostalgically towards their youth. For the young, the future seems to stretch forward to infinity. For the old, their past is fixed, there is no time to left to refashion it (*LV*, 399; *OA*, 377). Indeed, the self, the ego, becomes a past object, a congealed element of what Sartre had come to call the 'practico-inert', the congealed history of one's past actions and creations. Old age brings us face to face with our existence as we are for the other. Our internal self-image is constructed while we are young, and our bodies change gradually without this image of ourselves transforming. It comes as a shock when we suddenly find ourselves treated as old by others. Old age involves 'a dialectical relationship between my being for others, in so far as it is objectively determined, and the consciousness that I have of myself by means of it' (*LV*, 302; *OA*, 284). It is myself as I am for others that is old, and yet, that being that I am for others is myself. Actually, this kind of ambiguous situation is one that, according to Beauvoir's own philosophy, characterises our human condition. We are, at all periods of our life, both an internal consciousness of our bodily self and the exterior material being that exists for others. But Beauvoir suggests that the situation of being old has a particularly confronting character. Whereas one can challenge other images of the self that come from outside and refuse to identify with them, there is an undeniable biological reality to being sixty, seventy, or eighty years old that cannot be denied or overcome.

Yet, despite the pessimism and sense of being at the end of her life that exudes from her account of old age, Beauvoir's active life was by no means at an end. The generation who had been born while *The Second Sex* was gestating was coming of age. Twenty-one years after its publication, a spate of books appeared that, in one way or another, developed its ideas in a more radical, feminist direction. Shulamith Firestone's *The Dialectic of Sex*, Kate Millett's *Sexual Politics*, Germaine Greer's *The Female Eunuch*, and Robin Morgan's *Sisterhood is Powerful* all appeared in 1970, heralding the emergence of the women's liberation movement, and Beauvoir 'learnt with great pleasure that the new American feminism quotes *The Second Sex* as its authority' (*TCF*, 504; *ASD*, 455; Firestone, 1970; Greer, 1970; Millett, 1970; Morgan, 1970). Although she had not initially identified as a feminist and had taken the position that women would be liberated by a socialist revolution, during these last years she changed her attitude towards women's liberation and contributed actively to at least some feminist initiatives, particularly those aimed at the legalisation of abortion, a reform that she had already advocated in *The Second Sex* (*TCF*, 492; *ASD*, 444; Van Houten, 2015).

The last volume of her autobiography, *All Said and Done*, therefore adopts a more positive tone than the previous one. There is an element of a Sorites paradox about ageing. No single day can be said to mark the boundary between maturity and old age, yet at some point one is forced to accept that one has crossed over into a new status. Having accepted that she was old, Beauvoir ceased to feel as though she was ageing (*TCF*, 40; *ASD*, 30). The routine of her life went on as before: she continued to read, write, listen to music, and go to the cinema and theatre. There was also the gratification of new friendships, most significantly that with Sylvie le Bon Beauvoir, who was to become her literary executor and would be responsible for the publication and translation of the early diaries and essays that are now available (*TCF*, 68–74; *ASD*, 58–64). And she continued to travel, both for pleasure and as a result of the position that she and Sartre had obtained as celebrities of the 'New Left'.

She did not return to China and admits to having been unable to understand what was occurring while the Cultural Revolution was in full swing, when those of her acquaintances who had been there told her of the cult of Mao and the Little Red Book, which was constantly being waved about and read aloud over loudspeakers (*TCF*, 455–9; *ASD*, 411–15). She was sympathetic to its aim, as she understood it, of preventing a new privileged class from forming, but dismayed by the dogmatic naivety of the publications produced by the Chinese government. She was even more disillusioned with the USSR, which, in 1968, had sent tanks and troops into Czechoslovakia, thus quashing the movement towards a more liberal socialism that had proposed some workers' control over the management of factories. This occupation condemned writers who had been her friends to exile (*TCF*, 362–74; *ASD*, 325–37). Cuba, which, for a time, had represented 'the very embodiment of socialist hopes', had also disappointed, becoming dependent on the USSR and adopting its repressive policies (*TCF*, 453–4; *ASD*, 409–10). Yet the USA was acting in an equally intolerable manner by interfering in Vietnam to prevent the election of the government of a unified country, as had been agreed at the Geneva agreement of 1954 (*TCF*, 375; *ASD*, 334). From 1966 she and Sartre were closely involved in the unofficial trials, initiated by Bertrand Russell, set up to judge the USA on the count of committing war-crimes in Vietnam. The congresses that they supported and attended in Sweden and Denmark had a considerable impact as they were arenas for the dissemination of information about the atrocities being committed by the Americans and their allies and encouragment for the rising tide of moral condemnation against this unnecessary war (*TCF*, 379–403; *ASD*, 338–64). Beauvoir was as condemnatory of the unconscionable interference of the USA in the affairs of Latin America, which resulted in the military dictatorships of Brazil and Argentina and, a little after she had completed her memoir, of Chile (*TCF*, 463–5; *ASD*, 418–20).

The conflict between Israelis and Palestinians left Beauvoir devastated (*TCF*, 403–449; *ASD*, 364–406). Having lived through the Second World War and seen the persecution of the Jews, she was sympathetic to their need for a secure homeland, yet she was also moved by the plight of the Arabs whom she met when she visited Israel not long before the 1967 war. Just prior to this visit, she and Sartre had been invited to Egypt by a close associate of President Nasser, where they had been officially fêted by the government and had met Palestinian refugees in Gaza. Beauvoir's existentialist humanism and liberal socialism left her impotent in the face of the fanatical resentment of the Arabs and Palestinians, who threatened to push the Jews into the sea, an attitude that she found even more distressing than the wary distrust of the Israelis, who discriminated against those Arabs who continued to live among them and resisted Sartre's advocacy of the return of at least some of the displaced. She finds the idea that Israel should 'vanish from the map of the world perfectly hateful' (*TCF*, 448; *ASD*, 405). At the same time, she is critical of Israel's policy, which she sees as insufficiently focussed on peace. Fifty years later, the situation is no better, and fanaticism on both sides has destroyed communities, cost thousands of lives, and infected the whole of the Middle East with a horrifying and self-destructive disease. Existentialist humanism can appear impotent in the face of the religious dogmatism, nationalist self-righteousness, and cynical trade in arms that now blights the whole region.

During her travels, Beauvoir took a particular interest in the situation of women. In Egypt she met with 'a very old lady' who had been 'the first to declare war on the veil before 1914' (*TCF,* 418; *ASD,* 377). Rather prematurely, a footnote tells us that this war has been won. She criticised the continuing inequality between men and women in Egypt, accusing men, in a lecture that she gave in Cairo, of 'behaving like feudalists, colonialists and racists towards women' (*TCF,* 419; *ASD,* 378). In Israel she also met with women who, despite the theoretical equality of men and women in the kibbutzim, complained that they were not treated equally, while some felt that the earlier generation of women had made a mistake in giving up their womanliness and would have preferred to have looked after their own children, rather than relinquishing them to communal care (*TCF,* 426–8; *ASD,* 385–7). In France, Beauvoir became involved with the women's liberation movement. Following Juliet Mitchell's *Woman's Estate*, she concluded that socialism by itself did not account for women's subordinate position, but she did not want to go so far as those who would accuse men of being oppressors (Mitchell, 1971). She rejected feminist separatism and hatred of men, while endorsing Firestone's critique of the family (*TCF,* 506–8; *ASD,* 456–9). She also confirmed the social constructivist interpretation that 'one is not born a woman', adding to it the observation that it is also true that 'one is not born a man' (*TCF,* 497; *ASD,* 445). She was pleased that her work had had an impact, but in many ways her feminist legacy was one of confusion. As a result, subsequent writers were to extend her ideas in various conflicting directions.

5 Beauvoir's Impact

It is as a result of *The Second Sex* that Beauvoir has had the greatest impact on subsequent social and political movements, but its influence is both ambiguous and contested. Few feminists identify as existentialists, and Beauvoir's insistence that she had adopted a great deal of Sartre's existentialism as her own has been difficult for some to swallow (Le Dœuff, 1980; 1990, 164–5; Simons, 1986). Yet, even as they explicitly distance themselves from her, subsequent writers in the feminist tradition have adopted and developed methods and concepts that she pioneered. By fusing the interior perspective of existentialist phenomenology with the exterior analysis of social relations offered by Marxists, Beauvoir facilitated the turn towards 'feminist consciousness raising' and the articulation by women of their personal experience of oppression (Marks, 1986). Her proposition that woman is the Other of man feeds into accounts of sexual objectification and continues to have an enormous influence on feminist discourse. Her philosophy, as we have seen, was one of ambiguity, so that different interpreters have taken up different aspects of her work, developing them in their own way. At least some of the roots of quite different forms of feminist thinking can be traced back to her writing.

There are, indeed, two Simone de Beauvoirs. One, the author of *The Second Sex*, represents women as the Other of man, a dependent consciousnesses, constrained by social conventions to represent themselves to themselves through the eyes of men, who transform women into objects and confine them to a socially inferior status. The other, the author of the autobiographies, represents herself as an independent individual who may, from time to time, have been tempted to become emotionally dependent on some other, but who courageously carved out a career for herself and enjoyed a series of egalitarian sexual and personal relationships with men who treated her as their intellectual collaborator and equal, the most important of these being Sartre. The second Beauvoir operates as something of a pragmatic contradiction of the first. She wrote an account of women's situation that apparently did not apply to her. One can reconcile these conflicting stories by reading *The Second Sex* as an account of the past and a call for the transformation of society, so that women can come to experience themselves as authentic, transcendent consciousnesses, as she had managed to do. Both Beauvoirs had an impact: the first on the content of later feminist writings, the second as a transformative example to be emulated (Brock, 2016, 163).

Betty Friedan, who was one of the earliest authors to have been influenced by her, took up the call to question social expectations and learnt from her analysis. Friedan's *Feminine Mystique* of 1963 had a far greater impact in America than *The Second Sex* had done in either France or in America, where the first English translation had appeared ten years earlier (Brock, 2016, 54–7, 68, 160; Friedan, 1963). However, Friedan did not acknowledge her debt to Beauvoir until 1975. It was, she then admitted, *The Second Sex* that had introduced her to 'an existentialist approach to reality and political responsibility' (Dijkstra, 1980; Friedan, 1975, 16). In particular, Beauvoir's description of housework as being like the labours of Sisyphus resonated with Friedan, an American housewife for whom motherhood, children, and housework had become less than completely fulfilling. Although Beauvoir called *The Feminine Mystique* 'an excellent book', by 1975, when she and Friedan met, it was clear that their politics were fundamentally opposed (*TCF*, 502; *ASD*, 453). Friedan was interested in choice, in wages for housework, and in finding ways in which women's traditional domestic labour could be valued. Beauvoir was far more sympathetic to radical proposals, such as those developed by Firestone to abolish traditional motherhood and the family, (*TCF*, 506; *ASD*, 457). Friedan wanted women to achieve equality of opportunity, within the relatively inegalitarian, liberal democracy of the USA. Beauvoir wanted to abolish both economic inequality and traditional sex roles, approving of that strand of feminism that attempted to avoid traditional politics, which she now deemed 'a men's fight' (Beauvoir & Friedan, 1975, 56). For Beauvoir, Friedan's aspirations must have smacked too much of those of the successful woman who invested in a consumerist society, critically portrayed in *Les Belles Images* (Vintges, 2017, 21–4; *BI*, *BIe*). Though they managed to remain polite, it is clear from their exchange that, by 1975, they shared little common ground (Beauvoir & Friedan, 1975).

This mix of influence and opposition is also characteristic of the impact Beauvoir had on later French feminists. Irigaray's treatment of woman as 'the other of the same' clearly has roots in Beauvoir's characterisation of woman as Other. Indeed, she sent Beauvoir a copy of *Speculum of the Other Woman* when it first appeared and was disappointed that Beauvoir did not acknowledge the gift (Green, 2001; Irigaray, 1991, 31). Beauvoir had argued that men are transcendent subjects who have made women their Other. She had assumed that women could equally achieve transcendence. Irigaray demurred. She accepted with Beauvoir that 'We can assume that any theory of the subject has always been appropriated by the "masculine"'. But she concluded that when a woman sees herself as transcendent, she 'fails to realize that she is renouncing the specificity of her own relationship to the imaginary. Subjecting herself to objectivization in discourse – by being "female". Re-objectifying her own self whenever she claims to identify herself as a masculine subject' (Irigaray, 1985a, 133). If 'woman' and 'femininity' are nothing but male myths, as Beauvoir had postulated, an individual female will simply be succumbing to masculine ideology, in so far as she identifies with this mythic character. But, as Irigaray recognises, Beauvoir's own account of the masculine origins of culture suggests that the free transcendent male is equally a mythic construct of the masculine imaginary, making it just as problematic as an identification for women. The point had already been anticipated in *The Second Sex*, where Beauvoir suggests that both 'playing at being a man' and at being a woman, that is as being an object, the Other, are two kinds of self-alienation (*DS*, I.1.ii, 96; *SSp*, 77; *SSbm*, 61). But Irigaray's response, which is to attempt to find an authentic feminine language in the disruption of the symbolic order, is not one with which Beauvoir sympathised. It results from a strange hybridisation of Beauvoir's 'woman is the Other of man' with structuralism and in an adaptation of Lacan's structuralist Freud, which emerged in France during the 1970s (Whitford, 1991, 53–74).

'Women have always been defined in relation to men', claim Elaine Marks and Isabelle de Courtivron in their introduction to the influential anthology *New French Feminisms*, which includes a reprinting of the introduction to *The Second Sex* (Courtivron & Marks, 1985, 4, 41–56). They do not bother to cite

Beauvoir as their authority for this claim, which, in their version, now takes on a linguistic caste: 'a polarity of opposites based on sexual analogy organizes our language and through it directs our manner of perceiving the world' (Courtivron & Marks, 1985, 4). They accord Beauvoir an exemplary place within French feminism, reading her as having argued that 'all systems were biased because they were limited, because from the beginning of history women had been left out' (Courtivron & Marks, 1985, 8). The significance of Beauvoir's 'women have no history of their own' is now read in the light of 'the structuralist assault on the existentialist I'. She had assumed direct knowledge of a lucid consciousness, condemned to freedom. The structuralism that she had helped to popularise by promoting Lévi-Strauss disagreed. It deemed the free conscious self to be an illusion, an introjection of language, a symbolic system, imposed on the individual from without. In Lacan's structuralist reading of Freud, the privileged signifier in this symbolic system is the phallus: a masculine sexual signifier in relation to which the feminine sex is a lack. Read through such structuralist prisms, Beauvoir's position came to imply that 'there can be no revolution without the disruption of the symbolic order' (Courtivron & Marks, 1985, 30–2).[8] Or, perhaps, more bleakly, there can be no revolution. The whole enlightenment tradition of an interior self, oppressed by wicked others and seeking to liberate itself towards a realm of freedom, dissolves in the face of the supreme power now accorded to the sign.

It is not only the radical French feminists anthologised by Marks and de Courtivron who owe a great deal to Beauvoir, while going beyond her. The same is true of English-speaking feminists, first in the popular works of the 1970s and later in the academy. Just one year after *New French Feminisms* was published, the journal *Yale French Studies* devoted a special issue to Beauvoir's ideas, which contained, as well as articles by Marks and de Courtivron, one by Judith Butler and another by Margaret Simons, each of which anticipated two of the directions in which Beauvoir's impact would be felt over the next decades (Butler, 1986; Courtivron, 1986; Marks, 1986; Simons, 1986). Simons embarked on the quest to read Beauvoir independently of Sartre. Butler initiated a radical reconceptualisation of gender that would lead to *Gender Trouble* and the ongoing movement that attempts to disrupt gender dualisms (Butler, 1990). Reading Beauvoir's 'one is not born but rather becomes a woman' as distinguishing sex from gender – a distinction that Beauvoir did not, in fact, make – Butler, unlike most of those who read this sentence, was sensitive to the existentialist and productive element of choice in Beauvoir's philosophy. The

---

[8] Often, the 'new French feminists' are interpreted as rejecting Beauvoir's philosophy (Gross, 1990; Kaufmann, 1986). As Marks and de Courtivron show, their 'going beyond' her has deep roots in her writing.

female body becomes 'the arbitrary locus for the gender "woman", and there is no reason to preclude the possibility of that body becoming the locus of other constructions of gender' (Butler, 1990, 35). Whereas Le Dœuff had criticised that element in Beauvoir's 'one becomes a woman' that imbues it with choice, the attribution of bad faith, and the possibility that a woman might be responsible for taking the 'easy path' of dependence and irresponsibility, Butler reads her more positively as offering an analysis with emancipatory potential (Butler, 1990, 41; Le Dœuff, 1980). She does not accept that to pursue transcendence is 'masculine', involving an attempted transcendence of the body. Noting that for Beauvoir consciousness is always consciousness of the body, an insurmountable element of the human situation, she proposes that in fact Beauvoir wants to suggest an alternative to 'the gender polarity of masculine disembodiment and feminine enslavement to the body' so that 'to the extent that gender norms function under the aegis of social constraints, the reinterpretation of those norms through the proliferation and variation of corporeal styles becomes a very concrete and accessible way of politicizing personal life' (Butler, 1990, 45). Now, since there is no natural body, the sex/gender distinction collapses, sexual difference is itself socially constructed, and the mythic nature of natural sex is exposed. Endorsing Monique Wittig and Michel Foucault's rather different writings, she finds that 'the political uses of biological discriminations in establishing a compulsory binary gender system' is already implicit in Beauvoir's existentialism (Butler, 1990, 45; Foucault, 1984; Wittig, 1992).

It is the fate of every great and seminal philosopher to be developed in various directions by succeeding generations, in ways that deform and distort their original texts and intentions. The fate of Beauvoir's most influential work attests to the fact that, despite her own reservations in this regard, she was a philosopher. Her ideas have been expropriated by many different descendants and transplanted into new soils, resulting in hybrids that she might well not have recognised. Emerging out of the heavily Cartesian, French philosophical tradition that dominated her early twentieth-century education, she was torn between solipsism and a romantic desire to merge with some other: God or a perfect lover. Her egoism 'I shall take myself as an end' stood her in good stead in the competitive intellectual atmosphere of her student years (*CJ*, May 21, 1927, 348; *DPS*, 262). Except for Zaza and Simone Weil, she was not greatly impressed by her female contemporaries and found many women stifling and conventional. In Sartre she discovered a lover who lived up to her own high self-estimation, a man who was her equal, whom she never betrayed intellectually, since to have done so would have been a self-betrayal. She was a woman and a transcendent being who wanted to be a writer and who, indeed, became one.

When she came to write *The Second Sex*, she encountered women as relative beings, mostly described by the pens of men, for whom women are an alien sex. Women, it seemed, had failed to leave a lasting mark on culture – their preoccupations, when they wrote, were deemed vain and self-centred. Hegel's dialectic offered a compelling original schema within which to account for this cultural inferiority. The situation she described, in which men were the orchestrators of culture and women found themselves subordinate, dependent creatures, at best acolytes or muses of male genius, spoke to women of the generations that followed. Yet it was never a particularly satisfactory account of the situation it purported to explain – the supposition that women had always been subject to men – for it assumed the truth of female cultural impotence, accepting the reliability of man-made history. The marriage of the thesis that men had experienced themselves as transcendent subjects, whereas women experienced themselves as objects, with structuralist and social constructivist assumptions subsequently resulted in an unbridgeable impasse. Beauvoir had believed in authenticity, in both transcendence and bodily reality. But without bodily reality, there turns out to be nothing for women to be, apart from society's 'proliferation and variation of corporeal styles'. Irigaray may have attempted to find an authentic, material, feminine signifier in the 'two lips' of the female body, but Butler responds that the figure of materiality is itself already sexed (Butler, 1994). Individuals with male bodies can be women, those with female ones, men. Yet, without biology there is no unity among women, so that the prospects for women – divided by history, skin colour, class, caste, nationality, religion, family, and ethnicity – of finding an authentic 'we' are dim (Green, 1999).

Despite the inroads of structuralism and post-structuralism, there are those who still find her 'phenomenological' method relevant. This places her work within a broad community of feminist phenomenologists, some of whose aims and presuppositions were very distant from hers (Bergoffen, 1997; Stoller, 2017). Yet, although influenced by existentialism and phenomenology, Beauvoir was an eclectic thinker who was happy to draw on ideas gleaned from structuralism, Marxism, and psychoanalysis – incompatible philosophies that she wove together into her own original syntheses. She did not attempt to reconcile the conflicts among them into a single coherent system, which prevented her from claiming to be a philosopher. From a less rigorous perspective she certainly was one, but the eclecticism of her method and its development over time means that she does not fit neatly into any traditional school.

Beauvoir's impact has been considerable, but it points in various directions, and what her lasting legacy will be remains undetermined. Formed in the context of existentialist phenomenology and Marxism, her ideas took root as a structuralist and post-structuralist wave swept up her interpreters. Her feminist descendants have accepted her thesis that woman is the Other of man, often reading it as though it can still be sustained without assuming her expropriation of the Hegelian conflict between consciousnesses. But, if the sovereign consciousness of Descartes is a myth, if the free conscious subject is an illusion, then the sovereign subjectivity of men, and the conflict that is supposed to arise when one consciousness is objectified by another, is also a myth. Beauvoir's key to the mystery can then unlock nothing. Men and women must equally be prisoners of language. Individual men can no more be free sovereign subjects than women, no matter what stories they have told themselves. The dominance of men will reside merely in the dominance of their weapons and their texts in the history of our culture, and the female subject will have already emerged, in so far as she has articulated herself in the rich history of her texts. Thus, the turn to the history of women's philosophical and political writings that has taken place over the past three decades can also be recognised as a legacy of Beauvoir's Hegelianism, but one that rejects the fundamental male myth to which Beauvoir succumbed: the idea that woman is somehow a less self-conscious, self-articulating, linguistic being than is man (Broad & Green, 2009; Broad et al, 2006; Green, 1995; 2014; 2020; Waithe, 1987–95).

Abbreviations of Works by Beauvoir

ADD   *America Day by Day.* Translated by Carol Cosman, Berkeley: University of California Press, 1999.

ASD   *All Said and Done.* Translated by Patrick O'Brian with an Introduction by Toril Moi, New York: Paragon, 1993.

BI   *Les Belles Images.* Paris: Gallimard, 1966

BIe   *Les Belles Images.* Translated by Patrick O'Brian, London: Fontana Collins, 1969.

BO   *The Blood of Others.* Translated by Yvonne Moyse and Roger Senhouse, Harmondsworth: Penguin, 1964.

CJ   *Cahiers de Jeunesse, 1926–1930.* Edited by Sylvie le Bon de Beauvoir, Paris: Gallimard, 2008.

CS   *She Came to Stay.* Translated by Yvonne Moyse and Roger Senhouse, London: Flamingo, 1995.

DPS   *Diary of a Philosophy Student. Volume 1, 1926–27.* Translated by Barbara Klaw. Edited by Barbara Klaw, Sylvie Le Bon de Beauvoir, and Margaret A. Simons, Urbana: University of Illinois Press, 2006.

DPS2   *Diary of a Philosophy Student. Volume 2, 1928–29.* Edited by Barbara Klaw, Sylvie Le Bon de Beauvoir, Margaret A. Simons, and Marybeth Timmermann, Urbana: University of Illinois Press, 2019.

DS   *Le deuxième sexe* (1949), 2 Vols. Paris: Gallimard, 2nd edn. 1976.

EA   *The Ethics of Ambiguity.* Translated by Bernard Frechtman, New York: The Citadel Press, 1948.

FA   *La force de l'âge.* Paris: Gallimard, 1960.

FC   *Force of Circumstance.* Translated by Richard Howard, Harmondsworth: Penguin, 1968.

FCh   *La Force des Choses.* Paris: Gallimard, 1963.

FM   'La Femme et les mythes I, II, III'. *Les Temps Modernes* 3, XXXII, XXXIII (1947–49), 1921–43, 2199–24, *Les Temps Modernes* 4, XXXIV (1948), 62–95.

FR   *La femme rompue.* Paris: Gallimard, 1967.

FW   *Feminist Writings.* Edited by Margaret A. Simmons and Marybeth Timmermann, Urbana: University of Illinois Press, 2015.

Inv   *L'Invitée.* Paris: Gallimard, 1943.

LitM   'Littérature et Métaphysique'. *Les Temps Modernes* 1 (1946), 1153–63.

LitMe	'Literature and Metaphysics'. Translated by Veronique Zaytzeff and Frederick M. Morrison, in *PhilW*, 268–77.
LM	*Les Mandarins*. Paris: Gallimard, 1954.
LoM	*La Longue Marche*. Paris: Gallimard, 1957.
LoMe	*The Long March*. Translated by Austryn Wainhouse, London: André Deutsch and Weidenfeld & Nicholson, 1958.
LS	*Lettres à Sartre*. Paris: Gallimard, 1990.
LV	*La Veillesse*. Paris: Gallimard, 1970.
MA	*Pour une morale de l'ambiguïté*. Paris Gallimard, 1947.
MBS	'Must we Burn de Sade?' Translated by Annette Michelson, in *The Marquis de Sade: An essay by Simone de Beauvoir with selections from his writings* (London: John Calder, 1962).
MD	*Memoirs of a Dutiful Daughter*. Translated by James Kirkup, Harmondsworth: Penguin Books, 1963.
MJ	*Memoirs d'une jeune fille rangée*. Paris: Gallimard, 1958.
MM	*All Men are Mortal, a Novel*. Translated by Leonard Friedman, Cleveland: World Publishing Company, 1955.
MTD	*Une mort très douce*. Paris: Gallimard, 1964.
OA	*Old Age*. Translated by Patrick O'Brian, London: André Deutsch and Weidenfeld & Nicholson, 1972.
PC	*Pyrrhus and Cinéas*. Paris: Gallimard, 1944.
PCe	'Pyrrhus and Cineas'. Translated by Marybeth Timmermann and Stacy Keltner, in *PhilW*, 89–150.
PhilW	*Philosophical Writings*. Edited by Margaret A. Simmons and Marybeth Timmermann, Urbana: University of Illinois Press, 2004.
PL	*The Prime of Life*. Translated by Peter Green, Harmondsworth: Penguin, 1965.
PolW	*Political Writings*. Edited by Margaret A. Simmons and Marybeth Timmermann, Urbana: University of Illinois Press, 2012.
QS	*Quand prime le spirituel*. Paris: Gallimard, 1979.
RES	'A Review of *The Elementary Structures of Kinship*'. Translated by Veronique Zaytzeff and Frederick Morrison, in *FW*, 58–66.
SA	*Le Sang des autres: roman*, [Lausanne]: Marguerat, 1946.
SSbm	*The Second Sex*. Translated by Constance Borde and Sheila Malovany-Chevalier, London: Vintage Books, 2010.
SSp	*The Second Sex*. Translated by H. M. Parshley, London: Jonathan Cape, 1953.
TCF	*Tout compte fait*. Paris: Gallimard, 1972.
TM	*The mandarins: a novel*. Translated by Leonard Friedman, London: Collins, 1957.

THM   *Tous les hommes sont mortels: roman*. Paris: Gallimard, 1946.

VED   *A Very Easy Death*. Translated by Patrick O'Brian, Harmondsworth: Penguin, 1965.

WD   *Wartime Diary*. Translated by Anne Deing Codero, edited by Margaret Simons and Sylvie Le Bon de Beauvoir, Urbana: University of Illinois Press, 2009.

WDes   *The Woman Destroyed*. Translated by Patrick O'Brian, New York: Pantheon Books, 1969.

WS   *When Things of the Spirit Come First: Five Early Tales*. Translated by Patrick O'Brian, London: Deutsch, 1982.

References

Bainbrigge, S. (1995) A Crisis in Feminist Scholarship in France? Catherine Rihoit on Simone de Beauvoir. *Simone de Beauvoir Studies*, **12**, 159–61.

Bair, D. (1990) *Simone de Beauvoir. A Biography*. London: Jonathan Cape.

Barnes, H. (1959) *Humanistic Existentialism; The Literature of Possibility*. Lincoln: University of Nebraska Press.

(1998–9) The Question of Influence: Response to Margaret Simons. *Simone de Beauvoir Studies*, **15**, 40–7.

Bauer, N. (2001) *Simone de Beauvoir, Philosophy and Feminism*. New York: Columbia University Press.

Beauvoir, S. de & Friedan, B. (1975) Sex, Society, and the Female Dilemma: A Dialogue. *The Saturday Review*, **12–20**, 56.

Bell, D. (1983) *Daughters of the Dreaming*. Melbourne: McPhee Gribble/ George Allen and Unwin.

Benjamin, J. & Simons, M. A. (1999) Beauvoir Interview (1979), in Simons, M. A. (ed.), *Beauvoir and the Second Sex*. Lanham, MA: Rowman and Littlefield, 1–21.

Bergoffen, D. (1997) *The Philosophy of Simone de Beauvoir: Gendered Phenomenologies, Erotic Generosities*. Albany: State University of New York Press.

(2017) Of Women and Slaves, in Fielding, H. A. & Olkowski, D. (eds.), *Feminist Phenomenology Futures*. Bloomington: Indiana University Press, 101–24.

Blumenfeld-Kosinski, R. (ed.) (1998) *The Selected Writings of Christine de Pizan*. New York: W. W. Norton & Co.

Boethius (1999) *The Consolation of Philosophy*, trans. Watts, V. Harmondsworth: Penguin.

Bordo, S. (1987) *The Flight to Objectivity: Essays on Cartesianism and Culture*. Albany: State University of New York Press.

Broad, J. & Green, K. (2006) Fictions of a Feminine Philosophical Persona (or Philosophia Lost), in Condren, C., Gaukroger, S., & Hunter, I. (eds.), *The Philosopher in Early Modern Europe: The Nature of a Contested Identity*. Cambridge: Cambridge University Press, 229–53.

(2009) *A History of Women's Political Thought in Europe, 1400–1700*. Cambridge: Cambridge University Press.

Broad, J., Green, K., & Prosser, H. (2006) Emasculating Metaphor: Whither the Maleness of Reason? in Burns, L. (ed.), *Feminist Alliances*. Amsterdam: Rodopi, 91–108.

Brock, M. L. (2016) *Writing Feminist Lives. The Biographical Battles over Betty Friedan, Germaine Greer, Gloria Steinem, and Simone de Beauvoir.* Cham, Switzerland: Palgrave Macmillan.

Butler, J. (1986) Sex and Gender in Simone de Beauvoir's *Second Sex. Yale French Studies*, **72**, 35–49.

(1990) *Gender Trouble*. New York: Routledge.

(1994) Bodies that Matter, in Burke, C., Schor, N., & Whitford, M. (eds.), *Engaging with Irigaray*. New York: Columbia University Press, 141–73.

(2003) Beauvoir on Sade: Making Sexuality into an Ethic, in Card, C. (ed.), *The Cambridge Companion to Simone de Beauvoir*. Cambridge: Cambridge University Press, 168–88.

Cavendish, M. (1664) *Philosophical Letters*. London: n.p.

Courtivron, I. de (1986) From Bastard to Pilgrim: Rites and Writing for Madame. *Yale French Studies*, **72**, 133–48.

Courtivron, I.d. & Marks, E. (eds.) (1985) *New French Feminisms*. Brighton: The Harvester Press.

Curnow, M. C. (1975) *The Livre de la Cité des Dames of Christine de Pisan: A Critical Edition*. PhD. Vanderbilt University.

Daigle, C. (2017) Unweaving the Threads of Influence: Beauvoir and Sartre, in Hengehold, L. and Bauer, N. (eds.), *A Companion to Simone de Beauvoir*. Hoboken, NJ: Wiley Blackwell, 260–70.

Deutscher, P. (2017) Afterlives: Beauvoir's *Old Age* and the Intersections of *The Second Sex*, in Hengehold, L. & Bauer, N. (eds.), *A Companion to Simone de Beauvoir*. Hoboken, NJ: Wiley Blackwell, 438–48.

Dijkstra, S. (1980) Simone de Beauvoir and Betty Friedan: The Politics of Omission. *Feminist Studies*, **6**, 290–303.

Doran, R. (2013) 'Critique of Dialectical Reason' and the Debate with Lévi-Strauss. *Yale French Studies*, **123**, 41–62.

Dworkin, A. (1981) *Pornography: Men Possessing Women*. London: The Woman's Press.

(1987) *Intercourse*. New York: The Free Press.

Eaubonne, F. (1974) *Le féminisme ou la mort*. Paris: P. Horay.

Eribon, D. (1993) *Michel Foucault*, trans. Wing, B. London: Faber & Faber.

Firestone, S. (1970) *The Dialectic of Sex; The Case for Feminist Revolution*. New York: Morrow.

Foucault, M. (1984) *The History of Sexuality, 1*. Harmondsworth: Peregrine.

Friedan, B. (1963) *The Feminine Mystique*. New York: W.W. Norton & Company. (1975) No Gods, No Goddesses. *The Saturday Review*, 16–17.

Fullbrook, K. & Fullbrook, E. (1993) *Simone de Beauvoir and Jean-Paul Sartre: The Remaking of a Twentieth-Century Legend*. Hemel Hempstead, Herts.: Harvester Wheatsheaf.

Gines, K. T. (2010) Sartre, Beauvoir, and the Race/Gender Analogy. A Case for Black Feminist Philosophy, in Davidson, M., Gines, K. T., Marcano, D. L., Guy-Sheftall, B., and George Yancy, G. (eds.), *Convergences: Black Feminism and Continental Philosophy*. Albany: State University of New York Press, 35–51.

Gray, E. D. (1981) *Green Paradise Lost*. Wellesley, MA: Redoutable Press.

Green, K. (1994) Freud, Wollstonecraft, and Ecofeminism. *Environmental Ethics*, **16**, 117–34.

(1995) *The Woman of Reason. Feminism, Humanism, and Political Thought*. Cambridge: Polity.

(1999) Sartre and de Beauvoir on Freedom and Oppression, in Murphy, J. (ed.), *Feminist Interpretations of Jean-Paul Sartre*. University Park: Pennsylvania State University Press, 175–99.

(2000) De Sade, de Beauvoir, and Dworkin. *Australian Feminist Studies*, **15**, 69–80.

(2001) The Other as Another Other. *Hypatia*, **17**, 1–15.

(2014) *A History of Women's Political Thought in Europe, 1700–1800*. Cambridge: Cambridge University Press.

(2020) Reconsidering Beauvoir's Hegelianism, in Thorgeirsdottir, S. & Hagengruber, R. (eds.), *Methodological Reflections on Women's Contribution and Influence in the History of Philosophy*. Dordrecht: Springer, 113–24.

(2021) The Rights of Woman and the Equal Rights of Men. *Political Theory*, **49**, 403–30.

Green, K. & Roffey, N. (2008) Reconnaissance et le drame hégélien de la femme dans Le deuxième sexe, in Stauder, T. (ed.), *Simone de Beauvoir à cent ans de sa naissance*. Tübingen: Gunter Narr, 221–33.

(2010) Women, Hegel and Recognition in *The Second Sex*. *Hypatia*, **25**, 376–93.

Greer, G. (1970) *The Female Eunuch*. London: MacGibbon and Kee.

Gross, E. (1990) Philosophy, in Gunew, S. (ed.), *Feminist Knowledge: Critique and Construct*. London: Routledge, 147–74.

Halimi, G. (1962) *Djamila Boupacha*. Paris: Gallimard.

Hegel, G. W. F. (1977) *Hegel's Phenomenology of Spirit*, trans. Miller, A. V. Oxford: Clarendon Press.

Heidegger, M. (1962) *Being and Time*, trans. Macquarrie, J. & Robinson, E. Oxford: Basil Blackwell.

(1968) *Questions I et II*, trans. Alexos, K. et al. Paris: Gallimard.

Heinämaa, S. (2010) Phenomenologies of Mortality and Generativity, in Schott, R. M. (ed.), *Birth, Death, and Femininity: Philosophies of Embodiment*. Bloomington: Indiana University Press, 74–153.

Hrdy, S. (2000) *Mother Nature*. London: Vintage.

Imbert, C. (2004) Simone de Beauvoir: A Philosopher in the Context of Her Generation, in Grosholz, E. (ed.), *The Legacy of Simone de Beauvoir*. Oxford: Oxford University Press, 3–21.

Irigaray, L. (1985a) *Speculum of the Other Woman*, trans. Gill, G. Ithaca, NY: Cornell University Press.

(1985b) *This Sex Which is Not One*, trans. Porter, C. Ithaca, NY: Cornell University Press.

(1989) *Le Temps de la différence*. Paris: Livre de Poche.

(1991) Equal or Different? in Whitford, M. (ed.), *The Irigaray Reader*. Oxford: Basil Blackwell, 30–3.

(1993) *An Ethics of Sexual Difference*, trans. Burke, C. & Gill, G. C. Ithaca, NY: Cornell University Press.

Jeffreys, S. (1990) *Anticlimax*. London: The Women's Press.

Kaufmann, D. (1986) Simone de Beauvoir: Questions of Difference and Generation. *Yale French Studies*, **72**, 121–31.

Keralio-Robert, L.-F. (1786–9) *Collection des Meilleurs ouvrages François composés par des femmes, dédiée aux femmes françoises*, 14 vols. Paris: Lagrange.

Kirkpatrick, K. (2019) *Becoming Beauvoir: A Life*. New York: Bloomsbury Academic.

Kristeva, J. (2018) *Passions of Our Time*, trans. Borde C. & Malovany-Chevalier S. New York: Columbia University Press.

Kruks, S. (1991) Simone de Beauvoir: Teaching Sartre about Freedom, in Aronsen, R. & van den Hoven, A. (eds.), *Sartre Alive*. Detroit, MI: Wayne State University Press, 285–300.

(2012) *Simone de Beauvoir and the Politics of Ambiguity*. Oxford: Oxford University Press.

La Caze, M. (2004–5) Simone de Beauvoir: Freedom and the Scandal of Death. *Simone de Beauvoir Studies*, **21**, 142–54.

Le Dœuff, M. (1980) Simone de Beauvoir and Existentialism. *Feminist Studies*, **6**, 277–89.

(1990) *Hipparchia's Choice*, trans. Selous, T. Oxford: Basil Blackwell.

Lévi-Strauss, C. (1949) *Les Structures élémentaires de la parenté*. Paris: Presses universitaires de France.

(1966) *The Savage Mind*. Chicago, IL: University of Chicago Press.

Lloyd, G. (1984) *The Man of Reason: 'Male' and 'Female' in Western Philosophy*. London: Methuen.

(1986) Texts, Metaphors, and the Pretensions of Philosophy. *Monist*, **69**, 87–102.

Lundgren-Gothlin, E. (1996) *Sex and Existence: Simone de Beauvoir's 'The Second Sex'*, trans. Schenk, L. Hanover, NH: University Press of New England.

(2003) Reading Simone de Beauvoir with Martin Heidegger, in Card, C. (ed.), *The Cambridge Companion to Simone de Beauvoir*. Cambridge: Cambridge University Press, 45–65.

MacKinnon, C. (1987) *Feminism Unmodified*. Cambridge, MA: Harvard University Press.

Malinowski, B. (1937) *Sex and Repression in Savage Society*. London: Kegan Paul.

Mann, B. & Ferrari, M. (2017) *"On ne naît pas femme: on le devient." The Life of a Sentence*. Oxford: Oxford University Press.

Marks, E. (1986) Transgressing the (In)cont(in)ent Boundaries: The Body in Decline. *Yale French Studies*, **72**, 181–200.

McWeeny, J. (2017) Beauvoir and Merleau-Ponty, in Hengehold, L. and Bauer, N. (eds.), *A Companion to Simone de Beauvoir*. Hoboken, NJ: Wiley Blackwell, 211–23.

Mead, M. (1943) *Coming of Age in Samoa*. Harmondsworth: Penguin.

Merchant, C. (1981) *The Death of Nature: Women, Ecology and the Scientific Revolution*. San Francisco, CA: Harper and Row.

Millett, K. (1970) *Sexual Politics*. London: Rupert Hart-Davis.

Mitchell, J. (1971) *Woman's Estate*. Harmondsworth: Penguin.

Moi, T. (1994) *Simone de Beauvoir: The Making of an Intellectual Woman*. Oxford: Blackwell.

Morgan, R. (1970) *Sisterhood is Powerful: An Anthology of Writings from the Women's Liberation Movement*. New York: Random House.

Mussett, S. M. (2006) Conditions of Servitude: Women's Peculiar Role in the Master-Slave dialectic, in Simons, M. (ed.), *The Philosophy of Simone de Beauvoir: Critical Essays*. Bloomington: Indiana University Press, 276–93.

Myrdal, G. (1944) *An American Dilemma: The Negro Problem and Modern Democracy*. New York: Harper and Brothers.

O'Brien, M. (1981) *The Politics of Reproduction*. London: Routledge and Kegan Paul.

Offen, K. (2017) Before Beauvoir, Before Butler: "Genre" and "Gender" in France and the Anglo-American World, in Mann, B. & Ferrari, M. (eds.), *"On ne naît pas femme: on le devient": The Life of a Sentence*. Oxford: Oxford University Press, 11–36.

Pateman, C. (1988) *The Sexual Contract*. Cambridge: Polity.

Patterson, Y. A. (1989) *Simone de Beauvoir and the Demystification of Motherhood*. Ann Arbor, MI: UMI Research Press.

Perpich, D. (2017) Beauvoir's Legacy to the *Quartiers*: The Changing Face of French Feminism, in Hengehold, L. & Bauer, N. (eds.), *A Companion to Simone de Beauvoir*. Hoboken, NJ: Wiley Blackwell, 489–99.

Pizan, C. (1521) *The Boke of the Cyte of Ladies.*London: Henry Pepwell.

(1886) *Oeuvres Poétiques de Christine de Pisan*, 3 Vols., ed. Roy, M. Paris: Librarie de Firmin Didot et Cie.

(1936–40) *Le livre des fais et bonnes meurs du sage roy Charles V*, 2 Vols., ed. Solente, S. Paris: Champion.

(1983) *The Book of the City of Ladies*, trans. Richards, E. J. London: Picador.

(2001) *Le Livre de l'advision Cristine*. Paris: Champion.

Plumwood, V. (1989) Women, Humanity and Nature. *Radical Philosophy*, **52**, 16–24.

Rich, A. (1980) Compulsory Heterosexuality. *Signs*, **5**, 631–60.

Rivière, J. & Alain-Fournier (1926–1928) *Corrrespondence 1905–1914*, 4 Vols. Paris: Gallimard.

Rowley, H. (2005) *Tête-à-Tête: Simone de Beauvoir and Jean-Paul Sartre*. New York: Harper Collins.

Ruddick, S. (1990) *Maternal Thinking: Towards a Politics of Peace*. London: Women's Press.

Salleh, A. (1992) The Ecofeminist/Deep Ecology Debate. *Environmental Ethics*, **14**, 195–216.

Sanday, P. (1981) *Female Power and Male Dominance*. Cambridge: Cambridge University Press.

Sartre, J.-P. (1939) *Esquisse d'une théorie des émotions*. Paris: Hermann.

(1943) *L'être et le néant*. Paris: Gallimard.

(1962) *Sketch for a Theory of Emotions*, trans. Mairet, P. London: Methuen.

(1975) Existentialism is a Humanism, in Kaufmann, W. (ed.), *Existentialism from Dostoevsky to Sartre*. New York: New American Library, 345–69.

(1976) *Critique of Dialectical Reason*, trans. Sheridan-Smith, A. London: NLB.

(1992) *Notebooks for an Ethics*, trans. Pellauer, D. Chicago, IL: University of Chicago Press.

(1993) *Being and Nothingness*, trans. Barnes, H. London: Routledge.

(2004) *The Imaginary: A Phenomenological Psychology of the Imagination*, trans. Webber, J. London: Routledge.

(2012) *The Imagination*, trans. Williford, K. & Rudrauf, D. New York: Routledge.

Schopenhauer, A. (1958) *The World as Will and Representation*, trans. Payne, E. F. J. 2 Vols. Indian Hills, CO: The Falcon Wing Press.

Schwarzer, A. (1984) *After the "Second Sex": Conversations with Simone de Beauvoir*, trans. Howarth, M. New York: Pantheon Books.

Seigfried, C. H. (1984) Gender Specific Values. *The Philosophical Forum*, **15**, 425–42.

(1985) *Second Sex*, Second Thoughts. *Hypatia: Women's Studies International Forum*, **8**, 219–29.

Simons, M. A. (1986) Beauvoir and Sartre: The Philosophical Relationship. *Yale French Studies*, **72**, 165–79.

(1997) The Search for Beauvoir's Early Philosophy. *Simone de Beauvoir Studies*, **14**, 13–28.

(1999) Richard Wright, Simone de Beauvoir, and the *Second Sex*, in Simons, M. A. (ed.), *Simone de Beauvoir and the Second Sex*. Lanham, MA: Rowman and Littlefield, 167–84.

(2003) Bergson's Influence on Beauvoir's Philosophical Methodology, in Card, C. (ed.), *The Cambridge Companion to Simone de Beauvoir*. Cambridge: Cambridge University Press, 107–28.

Stawarska, B. (2020) Struggle and Violence: Entering the Dialectic with Frantz Fanon and Simone de Beauvoir, in Kistner, U. & Van Haute, P. (eds.), *Violence, Slavery and Freedom between Hegel and Fanon*. Johannesburg: Wits University Press, 93–115.

Stekel, W. (1943) *Frigidity in Woman, in Relation to Her Sex Life*, trans. Van Teslaar, J. S. New York: Liverright.

Stoller, S. (2014) *Simone de Beauvoir's Philosophy of Age: Gender, Ethics, and Time*. Berlin: De Gruyter.

(2017) What is Feminist Phenomenology?: Looking Backward and into the Future, in Fielding, H. A. & Olkowski, D. (eds.), *Feminist Phenomenology Futures*. Bloomington: Indiana University Press, 328–54.

Tidd, U. (2004) *Simone de Beauvoir*. New York: Routledge.

Van Houten, C. (2015) Simone de Beauvoir Abroad: Historicizing Maoism and the Women's Liberation Movement. *Comparative Literature Studies*, **52**, 112–29.

Vintges, K. (2017) *A New Dawn for the Second Sex. Women's Freedom Practices in World Perspective*. Amsterdam: Amsterdam University Press.

Wahl, J. (1951) *Le malheur de la conscience dans la philosophie de Hegel*, 2nd edition. Paris: Presses Universitaires de France.

Waithe, M. E. (1987–95) *A History of Women Philosophers*, 4 Vols. Dordrecht: Kluwer Academic Publishers.

Warren, K. (1990) The Power and Promise of Ecological Feminism. *Environmental Ethics*, **12**, 125–43.

Whitford, M. (1991) *Luce Irigaray, Philosophy in the Feminine*. London: Routledge.

Wittig, M. (1992) One Is Not Born a Woman, in *The Straight Mind and Other Essays*. Boston, MA: Beacon Press, 9–20.

Wollstonecraft, M. (1989) An Historical and Moral View of the Origin and Progress of the French Revolution and the Effect it Has Produced in Europe (1795), in Todd, J. M. & Butler, M. (eds.), *The Works of Mary Wollstonecraft*. London: Pickering and Chatto.

Cambridge Elements ≡

Women in the History of Philosophy

Jacqueline Broad
Monash University

Jacqueline Broad is Associate Professor of Philosophy at Monash University, Australia. Her area of expertise is early modern philosophy, with a special focus on seventeenth and eighteenth-century women philosophers. She is the author of *Women Philosophers of the Seventeenth Century* (CUP, 2002), *A History of Women's Political Thought in Europe, 1400–1700* (with Karen Green; CUP, 2009), and *The Philosophy of Mary Astell: An Early Modern Theory of Virtue* (OUP, 2015).

Advisory Board

Dirk Baltzly, *University of Tasmania*
Sandrine Bergès, *Bilkent University*
Marguerite Deslauriers, *McGill University*
Karen Green, *University of Melbourne*
Lisa Shapiro, *Simon Fraser University*
Emily Thomas, *Durham University*

About the Series

In this Cambridge Elements series, distinguished authors provide concise and structured introductions to a comprehensive range of prominent and lesser-known figures in the history of women's philosophical endeavour, from ancient times to the present day.

Cambridge Elements ≡

Women in the History of Philosophy

Elements in the Series

Pythagorean Women
Caterina Pellò

Frances Power Cobbe
Alison Stone

Olympe de Gouges
Sandrine Bergès

Simone de Beauvoir
Karen Green

A full series listing is available at: www.cambridge.org/EWHP

Printed in the United States
by Baker & Taylor Publisher Services